CRITICS ON YEATS

CRITICS ON YEATS

Readings in Literary Criticism

Edited by Raymond Cowell

Head of the English Department, Nottingham College of Education

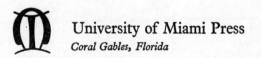

University of Miami Press

Coral Gables, Florida

CONTENTS

INTRODUCTION

Such was Yeats's capacity for 'remaking' his poetic self on the basis of rigorous self-criticism that any critic writing on his work before his death in 1939 is likely to be dismissed by us now—quite unfairly —as short-sighted. A frequent and amusing feature of critical comment on his work between the later 1890s and 1939 is the feeling that his latest publication is his worst. We should remember however that it cannot have been easy trying to evaluate such a restless talent and should therefore attribute the variety of estimates and interpretations of Yeats' poetry in these years less to critical obtuseness than to the difficulty and intricacy of Yeats' constant 'argument with himself'.

Though the recurrent note of slight uneasiness that characterizes the earliest comments can still be detected occasionally in the views of the revolutionary 'Modernists', the quality of critical comment takes a great leap forward in the second decade of this century. And the publication of *The Tower* in 1928 converted many previous sceptics so that John Gould Fletcher's review marks an important turning-point in the history of Yeats's reputation. It was published in *The Criterion* which was edited by T. S. Eliot.

The 1930s witnessed the emergence of literary criticism as a respectable and increasingly influential academic discipline and in 1931 there appeared in America *Axel's Castle* by Edmund Wilson, one of its finest practititoners, who presented Yeats as a poet who was extending and adapting French Symbolist theory and practice. In England, the Cambridge literary critical quarterly, *Scrutiny*, was becoming famous for its astringent 'revaluation' of established literary figures and in the early 1930s one of its editors, F. R. Leavis, presented Yeats as a victim of a degraded poetic tradition, a viewpoint elaborated in 1941—though in more specifically social terms—by another *Scrutiny* editor, L. C. Knights. In 1940, T. S. Eliot had withdrawn some of his earlier misgivings, admiring the sustained creative exploration of his own life that can be found in Yeats's poetry, and a similar emphasis on the coherence and unity of the poetry is prominent in an essay of 1942 by the American critic R. P. Blackmur. In fact, the immediately posthumous years saw no decline in Yeats's reputation such as sometimes follows the death of a great and influential poet and the emphasis in, for example, the essay by F. R. Higgins is on the work remaining to be done in placing the poetry in the right contexts.

With the exception of a major critical study by Macneice, the appearance of two biographies (by Hone and Jeffares) and a tribute from Auden, the later 1940s saw no very important contributions to Yeats criticism. The vastly larger part of the criticism quoted in the present volume comes from the 50s and 60s. Indeed it is only very recently that the earliest poetry has emerged from a fog of critical clichés about the 'Celtic Twilight'. Professor Daiches's essay suggests an essential continuity between this early work and the achievements of Yeats's later years and the essay by Daniel Hoffman on Yeats's use of the ballad form shows very clearly how much is gained from seeing Yeats's work as a whole. Wider continuities and parallels are suggested—though with a full awareness of the poet's originality—in Professor Kermode's study of his poetry in relation to earlier theories of 'the poetic image'. There is a danger, of course, that in studying the context of Yeats's poetry the critic might lose sight of the problems and challenges that are plausibly raised by some critics (Dr Leavis among them) when Yeats's ultimate status is being considered. Undoubtedly 'the Yeats industry' is sometimes guilty of myopic scholarship, mere source-detection, but, for example, Thomas Whitaker's reading of the difficult poem 'Meditations in Time of Civil War' shows a fine combination of unostentatious scholarship and critical sensitivity. There is no doubt that the reader looking for guidance on the poetry of Yeats's maturity is fortunate in having both the lightness of touch of Professor Donoghue and the meticulous scholarship of F. A. C. Wilson at his service. *Last Poems* is now beginning to attract close critical attention but the pioneer work in this field by Vivienne Koch, though occasionally marred by an excess of polemical fervour, has not yet been superseded.

It is surely not merely euphoric to think that Yeatsian studies are in a healthy state. The four general pieces on Yeats with which this volume ends are intended to prove the point. The unassertive scholarship of Bayley and Engelberg and the critical grasp of Ellmann and Lerner show that in the years between the late 50s and the present there has been no antagonism between 'critics' and 'scholars', as in some other fields of English studies. But then, great poems make good readers and if the best criticism is dialogue then it is no accident that the poet of 'A Dialogue of Self and Soul' has provoked some of the most interesting dialogue, discussion and disagreement in modern criticism.

Nottingham, 1971   *Raymond Cowell*

ACKNOWLEDGEMENTS

We are grateful to the following for permission to use copyright material from the works whose titles follow in brackets:

George Allen and Unwin Ltd and Harcourt Brace Jovanovich, Inc. (copyright, 1942, by Richard P. Blackmur. Reprinted from his volume *Language as Gesture* by permission of Harcourt Brace Jovanovich, Inc.); The Statesman and Nation Publishing Co. Ltd ('A Foreign Mind' from *The Athenaeum* of July 4, 1919); Jonathan Cape Ltd and Holt, Rinehart and Winston, Inc. (portion of a letter dated September 15, 1913 to Sidney Cox from *Selected Letters of Robert Frost*, edited by Lawrance Thompson. Copyright (c) 1964 by Holt, Rinehart and Winston, Inc. Reprinted by permission of Holt, Rinehart and Winston, Inc., Publishers, New York and the Estate of Robert Frost); Chatto and Windus (L. C. Knights's *Poetry as Social Criticism: The Work of W. B. Yeats*); The Society of Authors as the literary representative of the Estate of John Middleton Murry (John Middleton Murry's *Aspects of Literature*: 'Mr Yeats's Swan Song'); John Bayley (*The Romantic Survival*); J. M. Dent and Sons Ltd (Arthur Symons's *Studies in Prose and Verse*: 'Mr W. B. Yeats'); A. P. Watt and Son, M. B. Yeats and Anne Yeats (Preface to W. B. Yeats's *Ideas of Good and Evil*); Faber and Faber Ltd and New Directions Publishing Corp. (*The Literary Essays of Ezra Pound;* copyright 1918 by Ezra Pound. Reprinted by permission of New Directions Publishing Corporation, New York); Christy and Moore Ltd (letter dated June 30, 1921 from J. B. Yeats to W. B. Yeats); Faber and Faber Ltd and Farrar, Straus and Giroux, Inc. (T. S. Eliot's *On Poetry and Poets:* 'Yeats'); Faber and Faber Ltd and David Higham Associates Ltd (Louis Macneice's *The Poetry of W. B. Yeats*); Ernest Benn Ltd (John Eglinton, W. B. Yeats, A. E., W. Larminie: *Literary Ideals in Ireland*: 'Mr Yeats and Popular Poetry'); Victor Gollancz Ltd (F. A. C. Wilson's *W. B. Yeats and Tradition*); A. D. Peters and Co. (Denis Donoghue's *Yeats's Words for Music Perhaps*); Kennikat Press Inc. (F. R. Higgins's 'Yeats as an Irish Poet' from *W. B. Yeats: Essays in Tribute*, edited by Stephen Gwynn); The Bodley Head (William Archer's *Poets of the Younger Generation*); A. M. Heath and Co. Ltd and Diarmuid Russell (A. E.'s 'Imaginations and Reveries' from *A Poet of Shadows*); David Higham Associates Ltd and Oliver and Boyd Ltd (David Daiches's *Yeats's Earlier Poems: Some Themes and Patterns*); Oxford University Press by arrangement with the Society of Jesus (*Further Letters of G. M. Hopkins*, edited by C. C. Abbott); Oxford University Press (*Letters of Arnold Bennett*, vol. II, edited by J. Hepburn); Oxford University Press, Inc. (Daniel Hoffman's *Barbarous Knowledge: Myth in the Poetry of Yeats, Graves and Muir*. Copyright (c) 1967 by Daniel Hoffman. Reprinted by permission of Oxford University Press, Inc.); Oxford University Press, Inc. (Richard

Ellmann's *Eminent Domain: Yeats among Wilde, Joyce, Pound, Eliot and Auden*. Copyright (c) 1967 by Oxford University Press, Inc. Reprinted by permission); The British Academy (Laurence Lerner's *W. B. Yeats: Poet and Crank*); The Bodley Head and Houghton Mifflin Company (Archibald MacLeish's *Poetry and Experience*); Routledge and Kegan Paul Ltd (*W. B. Yeats and T. Sturge Moore: Their Correspondence*, edited by Ursula Bridge; Vivienne Koch's *W. B. Yeats: The Tragic Phase*; and Frank Kermode's *The Romantic Image*; Chilmark Press Inc. have raised no objection to the incorporation of this last-named extract); Martin Secker and Warburg Ltd (Forrest Reid's *W. B. Yeats: A Critical Study*); University of North Carolina Press (Thomas R. Whitaker's *Swan and Shadow: Yeats's Dialogue with History*); University of Toronto Press (Edward Engelberg's *The Vast Design: Patterns in W. B. Yeats's Aesthetic*. Copyright, Canada, 1964, by University of Toronto Press).

We have been unable to trace the copyright holders of the following two extracts, and would welcome any information which would enable us to do so. We are however grateful to Faber and Faber Ltd for their help with John Gould Fletcher's review of Yeats's *The Tower* in *The Criterion*, no. 30, September 1928; and to William Heinemann Ltd for their help with H. S. Krans's *William Butler Yeats and the Irish Literary Revival*.

Critics on Yeats
1886-1939

GERARD MANLEY HOPKINS (1844-89)

I called on his, young Yeats's, father by desire lately; he is a painter;
and with some emphasis of manner he presented me with *Mosada:
a Dramatic Poem* by W. B. Yeats, with a portrait of the author by
J. B. Yeats,[1] himself; the young man having finely cut intellectual
features and his father being a fine draughtsman. For a young man's
pamphlet this was something too much; but you will understand a
father's feeling. Now this *Mosada* I cannot think highly of, but I was
happily not required then to praise what presumably I had not then
read, and I had read and could praise another piece. It was a strained
and unworkable allegory about a young man and a sphinx on a rock
in the sea (how did they get there? what did they eat? and so on:
people think such criticisms very prosaic; but commonsense is never
out of place anywhere....)

> From a letter to Coventry Patmore, November 7, 1886, *Further
> Letters of Gerard Manley Hopkins*, edited by C. C. Abbott,
> London: Oxford University Press, 1938, pp. 225-6.

JOHN EGLINGTON (William Kirkpatrick Magee) (writing in 1899)

'I fear', said Blake to Crabb Robinson, 'that Wordsworth loves nature',
and Mr Yeats, as a philosopher, though not, we are glad to believe,
as a poet, would no doubt sympathize with that solicitude. The writer
whom he so greatly admires, Villiers de l'Isle Adam, cherished a
particular objection to the sun and daylight; and Paul Verlaine, whose
influence Mr Yeats would perhaps consider less baneful in this country than that of Wordsworth, acknowledged that he 'hated to hear the
laugh of a healthy man'. But really, what do the symbolists, who talk
so much of the 'exaltation of the senses' mean exactly by saying that
the 'poetic passion is not in nature', and that art is to be 'liberated
from life'. Life is nothing but what we make it, and we do not alter
its substance by twisting it into an abnormality. If the transcendent
realities do not exist in the normal human consciousness, they do
not exist in 'poetry, music, and painting', or at all. Mr Yeats thinks
that Shakespeare interested himself in life and humanity consciously

[1] John Butler Yeats, R.H.A. (1833-1922).

for the sake of his art. This is a matter of opinion; but we think it more likely that Shakespeare's interest in life was a broadly human and representative interest, and that this was the source and power of his art. Art which only interests itself in life and humanity for the sake of art may achieve the occult triumphs of the symbolist school, but humanity will return its indifference in kind, and leave it to the dignity and consolation of 'unpopularity'.

From 'Mr Yeats and Popular Poetry', John Eglinton, W. B. Yeats, A. E. and W. Larminie, *Literary Ideals in Ireland,* London: T. Fisher Unwin; Dublin: the Daily Express Office, 1899, pp. 41–6 (45–6).

ARNOLD BENNETT (1867-1931)

It dawns upon me that he is one of the men of the century, so aloof, so intensely spiritual, and with a style which is the last word of simplicity and natural refinement.

Letter to George Sturt, February 7, 1899, *Letters of Arnold Bennett,* edited by James Hepburn, Vol. II (1889–1915), London: Oxford University Press, 1968, p. 119.

WILLIAM ARCHER (1856-1924)

One other word, and I have done. It appears from the notes to *The Wind among the Reeds,* rather than from the poems themselves, that Mr Yeats is becoming more and more addicted to a petrified, fossil-ized symbolism, a system of hieroglyphs which may have had some inherent significance for their inventors, but which have now become matters of research, of speculation, of convention. I cannot but regard this tendency as ominous. His art cannot gain and may very easily lose by it. A conventional symbol may be of the greatest interest to the anthropologist or the antiquary; for the poet it can have no value. If a symbol does not spring spontaneously from his own imagination and express an analogy borne in upon his own spiritual perception, he may treasure it in his mental museum, but he ought not to let such a piece of inert matter cumber the seed-plot of his poetry.

From 'William Butler Yeats', *Poets of the Younger Generation,* London: John Lane, The Bodley Head, 1902, pp. 531–59 (556–7).

A.E. (George William Russell) (1867-1935)

I sigh sometimes thinking on the light dominion dreams have over the heart. We cannot hold a dream for long and that early joy of the poet in his new-found world has passed. It has seemed to him too luxuriant. He seeks for something more, and has tried to make its tropical tangle orthodox; and the glimmering waters and winds are no longer beautiful natural presences, but have become symbolic voices and preach obscurely some doctrine of their power to quench the light in the soul or to fan it to a brighter flame. I like their old voice-less motion and their natural wandering best and would rather roam in the bee-loud glade than under the boughs of beryl and chrysoberyl, where I am put to school to learn the significance of every jewel. I like that natural infinity which a prodigal beauty suggests more than that revealed in esoteric hieroglyphs, even though the writing be in precious stones. Sometimes I wonder whether that insatiable desire of the mind for something more than it has yet attained, which blows the perfume from every flower, and plucks the flower from every tree, and hews down every tree in the valley until it goes forth gnaw-ing itself in a last hunger, does not threaten all the cloudy turrets of the poet's soul. But whatever end or transformation or unveiling may happen, that which creates beauty must have beauty in its essence, and the soul must cast off many vestures before it comes to itself. We, all of us, poets, artists and musicians, who work in shadows, must some-time begin to work in substance, and why should we grieve if one labour ends and another begins?

From 'A Poet of Shadows', (1902), *Imaginations and Reveries,* Dublin and London: Maunsel and Company, n.d. (1918), pp. 24–8 (25–6).

JAMES JOYCE (1882-1941)

I [Yeats] had been looking over the proof sheets of this book one day in Dublin lately and thinking whether I should send it to the Dublin papers for review or not. I thought that I would not, for they would find nothing in it but a wicked theology, which I had probably never intended, and, it may be, found all the review on a single sentence. I was wondering how long I should be thought a preacher of reckless opinions and a disturber who carries in his hand the irresponsible torch of vain youth. I went out into the street and there a young man [James Joyce] came up to me and introduced himself. He told me he had written a book of prose essays or poems, and spoke to me of a common friend.

Yes, I recollected his name, for he had been to my friend [A.E.] who leads an even more reckless rebellion than I do, and had kept him up to the grey hours of the morning discussing philosophy. I asked him to come with me to the smoking room of a restaurant in O'Connell Street and read me a beautiful though immature and eccen-tric harmony of little prose descriptions and meditations. He had thrown over metrical form, he said, that he might get a form so fluent that it would respond to the motions of the spirit. I praised his work but he said, 'I really don't care whether you like what I am doing or not. It won't make the least difference to me. Indeed I don't know why I am reading to you.'

Then, putting down his book, he began to explain all his objections to everything I had ever done. Why had I concerned myself with politics, with folklore, with the historical setting of events, and so on? Above all why had I written about ideas, why had I condescended to make generalizations? These things were all the sign of the cooling of the iron, of the fading out of inspiration. I had been puzzled, but now I was confident again. He is from the Royal University, I thought, and he thinks that everything has been settled by Thomas Aquinas, so we need not trouble about it. I have met so many like him. He would probably review my book in the newspapers if I sent it there. But the next moment he spoke of a friend of mine [Aubrey Beardsley or Oscar Wilde] who after a wild life had turned Catholic on his deathbed. He said that he hoped his conversion was not sincere. He did not like to think that he had been untrue to himself at the end. No, I had not understood him yet.

I had been doing some little plays for our Irish theatre and had founded them all on emotions or stories that I had got out of folklore. He objected to these particularly and told me that I was deteriorating. I had told him that I had written these plays quite easily and he said that made it quite certain; his own little book owed nothing to anything but his own mind which was much nearer to God than folklore.

I took up the book and pointing to a thought said, 'You got that from somebody else who got it from the folk.' I felt exasperated and puzzled and walked up and down explaining the dependence of all good art on popular tradition. I said, 'The artist, when he has lived for a long time in his own mind with the example of other artists as deliberate as himself, gets into a world of ideas pure and simple. He becomes very highly individualized and at last by sheer pursuit of perfection becomes sterile. Folk imagination on the other hand creates endless images of which there are no ideas. Its stories ignore the moral law and every other law, they are successions of pictures like those seen by children in the fire. You find a type of these two kinds of invention, the invention of artists and the invention of the folk, in the civilization that comes from town and in the forms of life that one finds in the country. In the towns, especially in big towns like London, you don't find what old writers used to call the people; you find instead a few highly cultivated, highly perfected individual lives, and great multitudes who imitate them and cheapen them. You find, too, great capacity for doing all kinds of things, but an impulse towards creation which grows gradually weaker and weaker. In the country, on the other hand, I mean in Ireland and in places where the towns have not been able to call the tune, you find people who are hardly individualized to any great extent. They live through the same round of duty and they think about life and death as their fathers have told them, but in speech, in the telling of tales, in all that has to do with the play of imagery, they have an endless abundance. I have collected hundreds of stories and have had hundreds of stories collected for me, and if one leaves out certain set forms of tale not one story is like another. Everything seems possible to them, and because they can never be surprised, they imagine the most surprising things. The folk life, the country life, is nature with her abundance, but the art life, the town life, is the spirit which is sterile when it is not married to nature. The whole ugliness of the modern world has come from the spread of the towns and their ways of thought, and to bring back beauty we must marry the spirit and nature again. When the idea which comes from individual life marries the image that is born from the people, one gets great art, the art of Homer, and of Shakespeare, and of Chartres Cathedral.'

I looked at my young man. I thought, 'I have conquered him now,' but I was quite wrong. He merely said, 'Generalizations aren't made by poets; they are made by men of letters. They are no use.'

Presently he got up to go, and, as he was going out, he said, 'I am twenty. How old are you?' I told him, but I am afraid I said I was a year younger than I am. He said with a sigh, 'I thought as much. I have met you too late. You are too old.'

And now I am undecided as to whether I shall send this book to the Irish papers for review. The younger generation is knocking at my door as well as theirs.

Quoted in Richard Ellmann, *The Identity of Yeats*, London: Faber, 1954, pp. 86-9. A manuscript, intended as a preface to *Ideas of Good and Evil* (1903) but not published until after the poet's death, reprinted by permission of Mrs W. B. Yeats.

ARTHUR SYMONS (1865-1945)

But after all, though Mr Yeats will probably regret it, almost everything in his book can be perfectly understood by any poetically sensitive reader who has never heard of a single Irish legend, and who does not even glance at his notes. For he has made for himself a poetical style which is much more simple, as it is much more concise, than any prose style; and, in the final perfecting of his form, he has made for himself a rhythm which is more natural, more precise in its slow and wandering cadence, than any prose rhythm. It is a common mistake to suppose that poetry should be ornate and prose simple. It is prose that may often allow itself the relief of ornament; poetry, if it is to be of the finest quality, is bound to be simple, a mere breathing, in which individual words almost disappear into music.

Probably, to many people accustomed to the artificiality which they mistake for poetical style, and to the sing-song which they mistake for poetical rhythm, Mr Yeats' style, at its best, will seem a little bare, and his rhythm, at its best, a little uncertain. They will be astonished, perhaps not altogether pleased, at finding a poet who uses no inversions, who says in one line, as straightforward as prose, what most poets would dilute into a stanza, and who, in his music, replaces the aria by the recitative. How few, it annoys me to think, as I read over this simple and learned poetry, will realize the extraordinary art which has worked these tiny poems, which seem as free as waves, into a form at once so monumental and so alive! Here, at last, is poetry which has found for itself a new form, a form really modern, in its rejection of every artifice, its return to the natural chant out of which verse was evolved; and it expresses, with a passionate quietude, the elemental desire of humanity, the desire of love, the desire of wisdom, the desire of beauty.

From 'Mr W. B. Yeats', *Studies in Prose and Verse*, London: Dent, 1904, pp. 230–41 (234–5).

HORATIO SHEAFE KRANS (writing in 1905)

Nothing could serve better to bring into relief Mr Yeats's point of view and peculiar lyrical gifts than a comparison of his poetry with that of Mr Kipling. Mr Kipling, too often hard, flashy and materialistic, is the celebrator of imperialism. He loves the tumult of war and the din of labour, and sings of them with a rough and gusty energy, and in a language so plain that he who runs may read its whole meaning. He is too often an indifferent artist, speaking in the slang of the camp, and in accordance with the standards of the music-hall. Mr Yeats is the reverse of all this. He, and with him the men of the revival, stand opposed to the encroachments of a uniform civilization that is destructive of national and provincial variations of every kind. He shuns the distractions of the workaday world and courts the solitary delights of the spirit. His poems are full of thought, spirituality and lyrical phantasy, and have a music that is subtle, sweet and beguiling. They are the product of an exacting artistic conscience, and everywhere wrought with the utmost care. If Mr Kipling seeks too eagerly to catch the ear of the crowd, Mr Yeats tends, on the contrary, to address himself to a cult, that understands the content of his art and speaks its language.

From *William Butler Yeats and the Irish Literary Revival*, London: Heinemann, 1905, pp. 107–8.

ROBERT FROST (1874-1963)

'Who dreamed that beauty passes like a dream?' That line fairly weeps
defiance to the un-ideal, if you will understand what I mean by that.
The Rose of the World, The Fiddler of Dooney, The Lake Isle of
Innisfree, Down by the Sally Gardens, The Song of the Wandering
Aengus, the Song of the Sad Shepherd—those are all poems. One
is sure of them. They make the sense of beauty ache.

Then nowise worship dusty deeds.

Such an untamable spirit of poetry speaks there. You must really
read Yates. He is not always good. Not many of his longer things
are more than interesting. But the Land of Heart[']s Desire is lovely
and so is On Shadowy Waters in poetry and Cathleen Ni Hoolihan in
prose.
Some one the other day was deriving all the Masefield and Gibson
sort of thing from one line of Yates' Land of Heart[']s Desire:

The butter's at your elbow, Father Hart.

Oh Yates has undoubtedly been the man of the last twenty years in
English poetry. I won't say that he is quite great judged either by
the way he takes himself as an artist or by the work he has done.
I am afraid he has come just short of being. The thing you mention
has been against him. I shouldn't care so much—I shouldn't care
at all, if it hadn't touched and tainted his poetry. Let him be as affected
as he pleases if he will only write well. But you can't be affected and
write entirely well.

From a letter to Sidney Cox, c. September 15, 1913, *Selected
Letters of Robert Frost*, edited by Lawrance Thompson, London:
Jonathan Cape, 1965, pp. 93–4.

EZRA POUND (b. 1885)

I live, so far as possible, among that more intelligently active segment
of the race which is concerned with today and tomorrow; and, in
consequence of this, whenever I mention Mr Yeats I am apt to be
assailed with questions: 'Will Mr Yeats do anything more?', 'Is Yeats
in the movement?', 'How *can* the chap go on writing this sort of
thing?'
And to these inquiries I can only say that Mr Yeats' vitality is quite
unimpaired and that I dare say he'll do a good deal; and that up to
date no one has shown any disposition to supersede him as the best
poet in England, or any likelihood of doing so for some time; and that
after all Mr Yeats has brought a new music upon the harp, and that one
man seldom leads two movements to triumph, and that it is quite

B

enough that he should have brought in the sound of keening and the skirl of the Irish ballads, and driven out the sentimental cadence with memories of *The County of Mayo* and *The Coolun*; and that the production of good poetry is a very slow matter, and that, as touching the greatest of dead poets, many of them could easily have left that *magnam partem*, which keeps them with us, upon a single quire of foolscap or at most upon two; and that there is no need for a poet to repair each morning of his life to the *Piazza dei Signori* to turn a new sort of somersault; and that Mr Yeats is so assuredly an immortal that there is no need for him to recast his style to suit our winds of doctrine; and that, all these things being so, there is nevertheless a manifestly new note in his later work that they might do worse than attend to.

'Is Mr Yeats an Imagiste?' No, Mr Yeats is a symbolist, but he has written *des Images* as have many good poets before him; so that is nothing against him, and he has nothing against them (*les Imagistes*), at least so far as I know—except what he calls 'their devil's metres'.

He has written *des Images* in such poems as *Braseal and the Fisherman*; beginning, 'Though you hide in the ebb and flow of the pale tide when the moon has set'; and he has driven out the inversion and written with prose directness in such lyrics as, 'I heard the old men say everything alters'; and these things are not subject to a changing of the fashions.

From 'The Later Yeats', in *Literary Essays*, London: Faber and Faber, 1954, pp. 378–81 (378–9). The article originally appeared in *Poetry*, IV, II (May 1914) as a review of *Responsibilities*.

FORREST REID (1875-1947)

Now in Mr Yeats's work what we get is poetry and almost nothing but poetry. From beginning to end there is not even a momentary concession to those who demand anything else. Nor does he express in his poetry the thoughts and tendencies of his age, as Matthew Arnold and Tennyson expressed at least the religious thought of their time. Probably no poet has ever got into his work a more personal atmosphere. He seems not so much to look at the world as to brood over the images that are thrown from the world upon the mirror of his own soul. Nothing appears in his work that has not passed through and been transformed by his imagination. What we mean by style is, I suppose, only the more or less perfect expression of a writer's individuality, and the wonderful uniformity of spirit which reaches from book to book, and draws together all Mr Yeats's writings, making of them a kind of complete and rounded whole, is in great part the result of the undividedness of his personality, of a temperament that is amazingly self-centred. He is always himself. No one has ever worked with a more jealous care for his art and each rewriting of a poem has, at this time, almost invariably the effect of bringing it nearer to his own innermost vision. Hence it is that his work, as a rule, either strongly attracts or equally strongly repels. One may like it or one may not like it, but it would be difficult to remain untouched by it. Where it is accepted it becomes a part of life. It gives something that nothing else has ever given or can give. It blossoms and bears fruit: it has the profound influence of a deep spiritual experience.

And yet it stands, as I have said, extraordinarily outside the tendencies of an age whose art, too rarely touched by any desire for beauty, is becoming more and more controversial, more and more, in literature at least, the unwilling and ungrateful bondservant of movements social or economical, so that one chooses one's poet or one's novelist or one's dramatist as one chooses one's newspaper, for his opinions on politics, the relations of the sexes, socialism, the emancipation of women.

From *W. B. Yeats, A Critical Study*, London: Martin Secker, 1915, pp. 56–8.

JOHN MIDDLETON MURRY (1889-1957)

It may be that Mr Yeats has succumbed to the malady of a nation. We do not know whether such things are possible; we must consider him only in and for himself. From this angle we can regard him only as a poet whose creative vigour has failed him when he had to make the highest demands upon it. His sojourn in the world of the imagination, far from enriching his vision, has made it infinitely tenuous. Of this impoverishment, as of all else that has overtaken him, he is agonisedly aware.

> I would find by the edge of the water
> The collar-bone of a hare,
> Worn thin by the lapping of the water,
> And pierce it through with a gimlet, and stare
> At the old bitter world where they marry in
>   churches,
> And laugh over the untroubled water
> At all who marry in churches,
> Through the white thin bone of a hare.

Nothing there remains of the old bitter world, which for all its bitterness is a full world also; but nothing remains of the sweet world of imagination. Mr Yeats has made the tragic mistake of thinking that to contemplate it was sufficient. Had he been a great poet he would have made it his own, by forcing it into the fetters of speech. By re-creating it, he would have made it permanent; he would have built landmarks to guide him always back to where the effort of his

last discovery had ended. But now there remains nothing but a handful
of the symbols with which he was content:

> A Sphinx with woman breast and lion paw,
> A Buddha, hand at rest,
> Hand lifted up that blest;
> And right between these two a girl at play.

These are no more than the dry bones in the valley of Ezekiel, and,
alas! there is no prophetic fervour to make them live.

Whether Mr Yeats, by some grim fatality, mistook his phantasmagoria for the product of the creative imagination, or whether (as
we prefer to believe) he made an effort to discipline them to his poetic
purpose and failed, we cannot certainly say. Of this, however, we are
certain: that somehow, somewhere, there has been disaster. He is
empty, now. He has the apparatus of enchantment, but no potency in
his soul. He is forced to fall back upon the artistic honesty which has
never forsaken him. That it is an insufficient reserve let this passage
show:

> For those that love the world serve it in action,
> Grow rich, popular, and full of influence,
> And should they paint or write still it is action:
> The struggle of the fly in marmalade.
> The rhetorician would deceive his neighbours,
> The sentimentalist himself; while art
> Is but a vision of reality....

Mr Yeats is neither rhetorician nor sentimentalist. He is by structure
and impulse an artist. But structure and impulse are not enough.
Passionate apprehension must be added to them. Because this is lack-
ing in Mr Yeats those lines, concerned though they are with things
he holds most dear, are prose and not poetry.

From 'Mr Yeats's Swan Song', (1919) *Aspects of Literature*, London:
Collins, 1920, pp. 39–45 (43–5). A review of *The Wild Swans at Coole*.

T. S. ELIOT (1888-1965)

Mr Yeats, more than any of the subjects that have engaged his
attention, is what engages our attention in this book. When we read
it we are confirmed in the conviction—confirmed in a baffling and dis-
turbing conviction—that its author, as much in his prose as in his verse,
is not 'of this world'—*this* world, of course, being our visible planet
with whatever our theology or myth may conceive as below or above
it. And Mr Yeats's cosmos is not a French world, certainly. The
difference between his world and ours is so complete as to seem almost
a physiological variety, different nerves and senses. It is, therefore,
allowable to imagine that the difference is not only personal, but

national. If it were merely personal, it might be located, attached to ourselves as some eccentricity of our nature; but Mr Yeats is not an eccentric. He eludes that kind of relationship to the comprehensible. Everywhere the difference is slight, but thorough. For when we say 'not of this world', we do not point to another. Ghosts, mediums, leprechauns, sprites, are only a few of the elements in Mr Yeats's population, and in this volume they hardly appear at all. Mr Yeats cannot be localized as a *rond de cuir* of séances. When an Englishman explores the mysteries of the Cabala, one knows one's opinion of him, but Mr Yeats on any subject is a cause of bewilderment and distress. The sprites are not unacceptable, but Mr Yeats's daily world, the world which admits these monsters without astonishment, which views them more familiarly than Commercial Road views a Lascar—this is the unknown and unknowable. Mr Yeats's mind is a mind in some way independent of experience; and anything that occurs in that mind is of equal importance. It is a mind in which perception of fact, and feeling and thinking are all a little different from ours. In Mr Yeats's verse, in particular, the qualities can by no means be defined as mere attenuations and faintnesses. When it is compared with the work of any English bard of apparently equivalent thinness, the result is that the English work in question *is* thin; you can point to something which it ought to be and is not; but of Mr Yeats you cannot say finally that he lacks feeling. He does not pretend to more feeling than he has, perhaps he has a great deal; it is not feeling that standards can measure as passionate or insipid.

A review of *The Cutting of an Agate* from 'A Foreign Mind', *The Athenaeum*, July 4, 1919, pp. 552-3 (552).

J. B. YEATS (1839-1922)

... When is your poetry at its best? I challenge all the critics if it is not when its wild spirit of your imagination is wedded to concrete fact. Had you stayed with me and not left me for Lady Gregory, and her friends and associations, you would have loved and adored concrete life for which as I know you have a real affection. What would have resulted? Realistic and poetical plays—poetry in closest and most intimate union with the positive realities and complexities of life. And that is the world that waits, so far in vain, its poet. I have always hoped and do still hope that your wife may do for you what I would have done. Not idea but the game of life should have been your preoccupation, as it was Shakespeare's and the old English writers', notably the kinglike Fielding. The moment you touch however lightly on concrete fact, how alert you are!

From a letter to his son, June 30, 1921, *J. B. Yeats: Letters to his Son W. B. Yeats and Others 1869-1922*, edited by Joseph Hone, London: Faber and Faber, pp. 280-1.

JOHN GOULD FLETCHER (1886-1950)

The aim of the better poetry produced today is probably more nearly towards a tempered and logically disciplined romanticism, than towards the classicism that various able critics (notably Mr Eliot) upheld so intelligently immediately after the close of the war. As against some of the more anarchic vagaries of the 'free-verse' and 'surrealist' school, we are witnessing a return to the old forms (more freely conceived however), but the *content* of poetry today is probably not very different after all from that which the great romantics discovered. We have shaken off some of their major illusions, such as that of the perfectibility *en masse* of the human kind (Shelley); the possibility of inventing a system of symbols that will define and describe all human activity (Blake); the complete welding together of poetic diction and common speech (Wordsworth). In return we have acquired a great concentration of material, so that we can produce effects of epic breadth and dramatic poignancy in a very few lines. We do not dissipate our substance in the monotonous, and in the end, purely meaningless reduplication of verbal effects practised by such figures as Swinburne; our horizon is at once wider, and more limited to its immediate results upon ourselves as participators in the life of today.

Take, for example, such a poet as Mr W. B. Yeats in his latest volume, *The Tower*. Here we have not a collection of anthology specimens, good or bad, but what is essentially a *Weltanschauung* worked out at high tension in poetic form. To Mr Yeats, the world of myth and legend and the world of objective fact are extraordinarily close to each other. He sees the whole of outward phenomena and the whole of subjective fantasy as being in some sense like the creation of man:

> Death and life were not
> Till man made up the whole,
> Made lock, stock and barrel
> Out of his bitter soul,
> Aye, sun and moon and star, all;
> And further add to that
> That being dead, we rise,
> Dream, and so create
> Translunar Paradise.

This attitude enables him to see Troy burning in a haystack set on fire, and old legends coming to life in the tumult and fury of Ireland torn by civil war. Yet in thus moving closer to the epic (and the best parts of his book are brief, concentrated epics) he has not overlooked his own beginnings which were lyric evocations of 'old mythologies', akin to Keats and Shelley. Thus the sensitive critic can find in him alike echoes of the old romantic yearning and subrational love for the undisciplined world of imagination, alongside of Greek epic fatalism of contemplation directed to the outer world of fact. He corresponds, or will correspond, when the true literary history of our epoch is written, to what we moderns mean by a great poet.

From a review of *The Tower*, *Criterion*, No. 30, September 1928, pp. 131–2.

T. STURGE MOORE (1870–1944)

(i) Have you read Santayana's *Platonism and the Spiritual Life*? He thinks the Indian philosophers the most spiritual, but his arguments leave me sceptical as to whether mere liberation from existence has any value or probability as a consummation. I prefer with Wittgenstein, whom I don't understand, to think that nothing at all can be said about ultimates, or reality in an ultimate sense. Anyway I can say nothing that approaches giving me satisfaction, nor am I satisfied by what others say. Your 'Sailing to Byzantium', magnificent as the first three stanzas are, lets me down in the fourth, as such a goldsmith's bird is as much nature as a man's body, especially if it only sings like Homer and Shakespeare of what is past or to come to Lords and Ladies.

(ii) My dear Sturge Moore,

Yes, I have decided to call the book *Byzantium*. I enclose the poem, from which the name is taken, hoping that it may suggest symbolism for the cover. The poem originates from a criticism of yours. You objected to the last verse of 'Sailing to Byzantium' because a bird made by a goldsmith was just as natural as anything else. That showed me that the idea needed exposition.

From a letter to Yeats of April 16, 1930 and Yeats's reply of October 4, 1930, *W. B. Yeats and T. Sturge Moore: Their Correspondence, 1901–1937*, edited by Ursula Bridge, London: Routledge and Kegan Paul, 1953, p. 162 and p. 164.

ARCHIBALD MACLEISH (b. 1892)

No, the problem is real and has been real in every country in the West, Russia included, Russia particularly included, ever since the industrial revolution and its consequences turned the old personal world in which the arts could live in public as well as in private into the impersonal world of the mass society, and it was not resolved for Yeats by his dream of a pre-Christian Ireland. Twenty years later in 1913 'romantic Ireland' was 'dead and gone': it was 'with O'Leary in the grave' and he was face to face with an actual Ireland, an Ireland with a middle class like any other, an Ireland with its fair share of the hatred, the lying, the greed and the hypocrisy which afflict us all. And face to face with that public reality he found himself face to face also with the problem of art he had dodged before—the problem most contemporary poets continue to dodge—the problem of the place of poetry in this unpleasant prospect. Being the man he was he faced it squarely, and faced it, moreover, in a poem, and published his poem ('The Grey Rock') precisely where it belonged, at the beginning of *Responsibilities,* with 'September 1913' and the rest of those political poems beside it.

From 'The Public World: Poems of Yeats', *Poetry and Experience,* Cambridge (U.S.A.): The Riverside Press, 1960, pp. 115-47 (133). An earlier form of this viewpoint appeared in the Spring 1938 issue of *The Yale Review* and was welcomed by Yeats.

Modern Critics on Yeats

F. R. HIGGINS

Yeats as an Irish Poet

Ireland was the moulder of Yeats's mind, as it eventually became the sounding-board for most of his verse and the great stimulating impact on his life. Throughout that intense life two men were his aristocratic heroes: John O'Leary and Parnell. On them he fashioned his heroic poise. For him one man typified the significant romanticism of Irish life; the other revealed its tragic realism. Yeats was the child of Parnell's race; the son by adoption of O'Leary's; but O'Leary's people— the Gaelic people, who lived dangerously to die jestfully—were his first and lasting influence.

From boyhood W. B. Yeats intimately knew his romantic and pastoral Sligo; later Clare-Galway became more attractive to the growing austerity of his mind. All through life his thought was never far from the West of Ireland. As a boy its quaint and adventurous folk, its grey fringes touching an uncharted world, were seen through 'magic casements'. His early verse—heavy with dream and frail reality— arises from these. That strange territory, that phantasmagoria, was his rich possession of poetry; and for it the English critics very quickly claimed a Celtic kingdom.

Yeats had thought to create a sensuous, musical vocabulary, to marshal the Irish fragmentary beauties into a great literature and indeed to give to Ireland a constantly artistic conscience through the medium of a poetic hierarchy. Until about 1907 all his achievements are towards that aim. Yeats, however, grew weary of his own ceremonial style—a style that seemed more concerned with cadence than content, of things imaged, as it were, through water. And away from the poetry of ornamental illumination, rather than flash, he hardened himself, subduing the lavish painting and toning down the rich sounds. He sought to rid himself of elaboration, of redundancy— through various ways. He found his new method by ballad-writing, for instance, and by writing out first in prose the substance of the verse on which he was working. He, however, succeeded mainly in his later work by the introduction of and tenacious adherence to stern theme and structure. With that success his poetry of mood gives way to his poetry of dramatic passion. It became hard-bitten: more Gaelic in feeling.

This change of his is due surely to what he heard and knew of Irish verse, traditional and translated, due possibly to the influence of Lady Gregory's mind and Synge's, as well as to a dramatic command and understanding of his craft. His early interest in bringing back poetry to its spoken majesty—a poetry as much for the ear as for the eye— was shown by his experiments in speaking verse to the psaltery. English poets were losing not only their ears but their mouths. They lolled their tongues in unmanly verse, seemingly anticipating the depression and defeatism of much verse in the England of today. Yeats was mainly interested in the lyric, in song. He had heard the ballad singers in fairs and markets crying out their pointed words of dramatic passion to catch and hold the ear of passing crowds. In street, field and kitchen Ireland was always singing in his youth, he recollec- ted; all the material for song was at his elbow. Ireland gave his splendid memory the songs of the folk; his friends gave him their translations from the Gaelic—precise, intense.

Snatches of these songs and poems were always running through his mind. Their phrases enter many poems by him. I remember him telling me some years back that most of his poems were composed to some vague tune, some lilt. Indeed, when we were together, he sang in his own uncertain, shy way, some of these poems. Whenever these poems were again repeated, at later dates, he always sang them to the same halting lilt. All poetry, Yeats frequently said, was song; and his *Oxford Book of Modern Verse* was largely compiled by him on that principle. In song-writing, Yeats took more than a literary interest. He wanted the songs of Irish poets sung among Irish people. In writ- ing his own songs, we worked together welding his occasionally meandering words to Gaelic tunes. That exercise was latterly his constant delight—an enthusiasm afterwards fructifying in our jointly edited volume of Broadsides made from Irish traditional songs, the songs of our friends, and our own songs. Convivial meetings of Irish poets should be the occasion for song production. It was a frequent idea; for him the social gatherings of the Irish Academy of Letters should take place in the upper room of some Dublin public-house, where the poets present would sing their own work. Such gatherings did take place, songs were sung, including Yeats's—but not in an actual public-house. Poetry must be brought to the people by song.

Yeats had no melodic ear; he could not measure words to musical stresses—he realized their significance, sought hard to employ them; but they were not at his ready command. The older musical scales, the Irish gapped scale with its dramatic possibilities, interested him; he abhorred the modern scale and the verbal contortions of concert singers. That very lack of a honied musical ear may have offered verbal compensation. It saves him, at worst, from an easy jingle of softly flowing sounds; from the monotonous regularity of well-timed stresses.

Indeed, his innocent offences against the laws of musical grammarians, his unconscious flaws in conventional melody, are responsible maybe for his curiously haunting harmonics in rhythm. These unexpected gaps staying his music, these hesitations in verbal sureness, dramatize his cadence. His carefully poised verse is tuned, as it were, slightly off the note. Throughout one listens as to a folk singer, in constant fear that the thin run of melody will break on the perilous top note—altogether a tantalizing music and a very personal music. Indeed, the very complex personality of this poet gave distinction to everything he wrote. His most formal lines, the most prosaic statement of his, stick in the mind, due possibly to such twist of syntax. Apart from such distinctiveness, the world of his mind, his imagination, circled far above the limp imagination of Main Street. His poetry never saw eye to eye with the middle classes. The bloodlessness, the loose sentiment of middle-minded verse, was to him an abhorrence. There were, for him, only two co-mingling states of verse. One, simple, bucolic, or rabelaisian, the other, intellectual, exotic, or visionary. The middle minds lacked distinction, poise; he had little interest or patience with them. To them his poetry may seem a beautiful secretion from a mind of aristocratic pedantry in which the insignificant is given an absurdly pontifical importance. Above them Yeats, however, nobly asserted his aloofness, striking home with a more telling, naked enterprise in Irish song—until he retired, as it were, into his own shell, but from there we hear the almost imperceptible music of a lost Kingdom.

From 'Yeats as Irish Poet', *William Butler Yeats: Essays in Tribute,* edited by Stephen Gwynn, New York: Kennikat Press, 1965, pp. 147–55 (147–53). This collection of tributes was originally published under the title *Scattering Branches* (1940).

L. C. KNIGHTS

A Heroic Failure

Perhaps the best way of defining the disappointment that one feels on returning to so many of Yeats's poems that had previously seemed deeply moving is to say that they fail to 'gather strength of life, with being', to grow, that is, with one's own developing experience,—unlike so much of Eliot's poetry where each fresh reading brings fresh discovery. For not only does Yeats tend to simplify his problems, there is in much of his poetry a static quality which can be traced to the adoption of certain fixed attitudes in the face of experience. 'There is a relation', he said, 'between discipline and the theatrical sense. . . . Active virtue as distinguished from the passive acceptance of a current code is therefore theatrical, consciously dramatic, the wearing of a mask.'[1] But his preoccupation with the mask was not merely a search for a discipline: sometimes it seems like the rationalization of a self-dramatizing egotism which made him feel happier if he could see himself ('Milton's Platonist') in an appropriate light. Consider, for example, his attitude of pride. One can relish his criticism of those who 'long for popularity that they may believe in themselves' and of poets who 'want marching feet', and at the same time recognize a danger to sincerity in a too persistent assertion of 'something steel-like and cold within the will, something passionate and cold.'[2] There is a smack of the Nineties here; and one remembers his fondness for Dowson's lines,

Unto us they belong,
  Us the bitter and gay,
Wine and women and song.

' "Bitter and gay", that is the heroic mood', he wrote in 1935. Like the aristocratic order that he imagined, pride is valued as an assertion of the living spirit confronted with democratic commonness; but there is something unliving in the use he makes of 'cold' and 'bitter' and 'proud'—adjectives that tend to appear with the same regularity as the 'emblems' which, in his later poetry, too often take the place of living metaphor. There is no doubt that the sap flows most freely when the conscious pride is forgotten, remaining only as a temper of mind that

[1] *Dramatis Personae*, p. 87. Compare p. 79 of the same volume ('Style, personality—deliberately adopted and therefore a mask—is the only escape from the hot-faced bargainers and the money-changers') and many passages in *Autobiographies*.

[2] The references are to *Dramatis Personae*, p. 84, and *Letters on Poetry*, p. 8.

is sufficiently assured not to insist on its own firmness. The pose that results from over-insistence is most obvious in admittedly minor poems, like the short sequence 'Upon a Dying Lady' and those verses that celebrate 'the discipline of the looking-glass', which he seems to have continued to regard as the appropriate discipline for beautiful women; but it also betrays itself in work of greater power. In the third section of the title poem of *The Tower* he writes of 'upstanding men',

> I declare
> They shall inherit my pride,
> The pride of people that were
> Bound neither to Cause nor to State,
> Neither to slaves that were spat on,
> Nor to the tyrants that spat,
> The people of Burke and of Grattan
> That gave, though free to refuse...

The rhythm of these lines seems almost mechanical when compared with the vigorous protest against old age with which the same poem opens. The pride, in short, sometimes seems like another form of the escape from complexity. Referring, once more, to the mask, he wrote: 'I think all happiness depends on the energy to assume the mask of some other self; that all joyous or creative life is a re-birth as something not oneself.... We put on a grotesque or solemn painted face to hide us from the terrors of judgment, invent an imaginative Saturnalia where one forgets reality, a game like that of a child, where one loses the infinite pain of self-realization.'[3] Yeats knew as well as anyone that 'the infinite pain of self-realization' is the price paid for 'life'; and in the lines that he wrote for his epitaph there is a deep and unintended pathos:

> Cast a cold eye
> On life, on death.
> Horseman, pass by.

This account, I know, ignores many fine poems—poems on 'that monstrous thing, returned yet unrequited love', and on the encroachment of age, some satiric pieces, and some others—and where much remains it must seem peculiarly ungrateful to insist on inadequacies and disappointments. But I hope I have made it plain that it is precisely because of his great qualities that one must judge Yeats's work, not simply in relation to the poetry of the late nineteenth century (his own included) but in the light of his own conception of the poet's function.

From 'Poetry and Social Criticism: The Work of W. B. Yeats' (1941), *Explorations*, London: Chatto and Windus, 1951, pp. 170–85 (177–9).

[3] *Dramatis Personae*, pp. 121–2.

T. S. ELIOT

The Poet of Middle Age

The points that I particularly wish to make about Yeats's development are two. The first, on which I have already touched, is that to have accomplished what Yeats did in the middle and later years is a great and permanent example—which poets-to-come should study with reverence—of what I have called Character of the Artist: a kind of moral, as well as intellectual, excellence. The second point, which follows naturally after what I have said in criticism of the lack of complete emotional expression in his early work, is that Yeats is pre-eminently the poet of middle age. By this I am far from meaning that he is a poet only for middle-aged readers: the attitude towards him of younger poets who write in English, the world over, is enough evidence to the contrary. Now, in theory, there is no reason why a poet's inspiration or material should fail, in middle age or at any time before senility. For a man who is capable of experience finds himself in a different world in every decade of his life; as he sees it with different eyes, the material of his art is continually renewed. But in fact, very few poets have shown this capacity of adaptation to the years. It requires, indeed, an exceptional honesty and courage to face the change. Most men either cling to the experiences of youth, so that their writing becomes an insincere mimicry of their earlier work, or they leave their passion behind, and write only from the head, with a hollow and wasted virtuosity. There is another and even worse temptation: that of becoming dignified, of becoming public figures with only a public existence—coat-racks hung with decorations and distinctions, doing, saying, and even thinking and feeling only what they believe the public expects of them. Yeats was not that kind of poet: and it is, perhaps, a reason why young men should find his later poetry more acceptable than older men easily can. For the young can see him as a poet who in his work remained in the best sense always young, who even in one sense became young as he aged. But the old, unless they are stirred to something of the honesty with oneself expressed in the poetry, will be shocked by such a revelation of what a man really is and remains. They will refuse to believe that *they* are like that.

> You think it horrible that lust and rage
> Should dance attendance upon my old age;
> They were not such a plague when I was young:
> What else have I to spur me into song?

These lines are very impressive and not very pleasant, and the sentiment has recently been criticized by an English critic whom I generally respect. But I think he misread them. I do not read them as a personal confession of a man who differed from other men, but of a man who was essentially the same as most other men; the only difference is in the greater clarity, honesty and vigour. To what honest man, old enough, can these sentiments be entirely alien? They can be subdued and disciplined by religion, but who can say that they are dead? Only those to whom the maxim of La Rochefoucauld applies: 'Quand les vices nous quittent, nous nous flattons de la créance que c'est nous qui les quittons.' The tragedy of Yeats's epigram is all in the last line.

Similarly, the play *Purgatory* is not very pleasant, either. There are aspects of it which I do not like myself. I wish he had not given it this title, because I cannot accept a purgatory in which there is no hint, or at least no emphasis upon Purgation. But, apart from the extraordinary theatrical skill with which he has put so much action within the compass of a very short scene of but little movement, the play gives a masterly exposition of the emotions of an old man. I think that the epigram I have just quoted seems to me just as much to be taken in a dramatic sense as the play *Purgatory*. The lyric poet—and Yeats was always lyric, even when dramatic—can speak for every man, or for men very different from himself; but to do this he must for the moment be able to identity himself with every man or other men; and it is only his imaginative power of becoming this that deceives some readers into thinking that he is speaking for and of himself alone —especially when they prefer not to be implicated.

I do not wish to emphasize this aspect only of Yeats's poetry of age. I would call attention to the beautiful poem in *The Winding Stair*, in memory of Eva Gore-Booth and Con Markiewicz, in which the picture at the beginning, of:

Two girls in silk kimonos, both
Beautiful, one a gazelle,

gets great intensity from the shock of the later line;

When withered, old and skeleton gaunt,

and also to 'Coole Park', beginning

I meditate upon a swallow's flight,
Upon an aged woman and her house.

In such poems one feels that the most lively and desirable emotions of youth have been preserved to receive their full and due expression in retrospect. For the interesting feelings of age are not just different feelings; they are feelings into which the feelings of youth are integrated.

From 'Yeats', (a lecture delivered at the Abbey Theatre in 1940), *On Poetry and Poets*, London: Faber and Faber, 1957, pp. 252–62 (256–9).

R. P. BLACKMUR

Four Aids to Navigation

So in Yeats, we can detach certain notions which we call basic—though we may mean only that they are detachable—as clues to better reading. At the end of the first version of *A Vision*, Yeats suggests the need of putting myths back into philosophy, and in the 'Dedication to Vestigia' in the same version, there is the following sentence: 'I wished for a system of thought that would leave my imagination free to create as it chose and yet make all that it created, or could create, part of the one history, and that the soul's.' If we take these two notions as sentiments, as unexpanded metaphors, we can understand both what drove Yeats to manufacture his complicated abstract system and the intensity of his effort to make over half of the consequent poetry as concrete as possible. He knew for himself as a poet that the most abstract philosophy or system must be *of* something, and that its purpose must be to liberate, to animate, to elucidate that something; and he knew further that that something must be somehow present in the philosophy. His system, if it worked, would liberate his imagination; and if it worked it must put those myths—the received forms, the symbolic versions of human wisdom—which were its object concretely into his system. A philosophy for poetry cannot be a rationale of meaning, but, in the end, a myth for the experience of it.

I should like to put beside these two notions or sentiments, two more. At different places in his autobiographies and in his letters to Dorothy Wellesley, Yeats quotes one or another version of Aristotle's remark that a poet should 'think like a wise man, yet express himself like the common people'. It should be insisted that this is a very different thing from what has been lately foisted on us as a model in the guise of Public Speech. To turn poetry into public speech is to turn it into rhetoric in the bad sense or sentimentality in the meretricious sense.

> The rhetorician would deceive his neighbours,
> The sentimentalist himself; while art
> Is but a vision of reality.

If we keep these lines—from one of Yeats's more esoteric poems—well in mind, they will explain for us much of what Yeats meant by the desire to express himself like the common people. He wanted to charge his words to the limit, or to use words that would take the maximum charge upon themselves, in such a way that they would be

c

available to the unlearned reader, and demand of him all those skills
of understanding that go without learning. We shall come to an example shortly.

The fourth sentiment that I want brought to mind here is again
one found in many places in both prose and verse in Yeats's work.
This is his sentiment that a poet writes out of his evil luck, writes
to express that which he is not and perforce, for completion or unity,
desires to be. Dante required his exile and beggary, the corruption
of the Church, the anarchy of Florence, in order to write *The Divine
Comedy*, with its vast ordering of emotion, its perspicuous judgment
of disorder and corruption. Villon needed his harlots and his cronies
at the gibbet. 'Such masters—Villon and Dante, let us say—would not,
when they speak through their art, change their luck; yet they are
mirrored in all the suffering of their desire. The two halves of their
nature are so completely joined that they seem to labour for their
objects, and yet to desire whatever happens, being at the same instant
predestinate and free, creation's very self.' So Yeats in his chapter
of autobiography called 'Hodos Chameliontos'—the path of muddle-
ment, of change, of shift from opposite to opposite. And he goes on,
in language characteristic elsewhere of his regard both for his own
life and his own works: 'We gaze at such men in awe, because we
gaze not at a work of art, but at the re-creation of the man through the
art, the birth of a new species of man, and it may even seem that the
hairs of our heads stand up, because that birth, that re-creation, is
from terror.' Lastly, in the next paragraph, there is a declaration of
exactly what I want to make manifest as the effort in the dramatically
phrased poems of the later years. 'They and their sort', he writes, and
it is still Dante and Villon, 'alone earn contemplation, for it is only
when the intellect has wrought the whole of life to drama, to crisis,
that we may live for contemplation, and yet keep our intensity.'

Now I do not believe Yeats felt all these sentiments all the time,
for a man is never more than partly himself at one time, and there is
besides a kind of outward buoyancy that keeps us up quite as much
as the inward drive keeps us going—but I believe that if we keep all
four sentiments pretty much consciously in mind we shall know very
nearly where we are in the simplest and most dramatic as in the most
difficult and most occult of Yeats's poems. With these sentiments
for landmarks, he is pretty sure to have taken a two- or a three- or
even occasionally a four-point bearing, in setting the course of a
particular poem.

To say this smacks of instruments and tables, of parallel rules and
compass roses. But only when the waters are strange and in thick
weather are thoughts taken as instruments necessary or helpful. With
familiarity the skill of knowledge becomes unconscious except in
analysis, running into the senses, and all seems plain sailing. As with
sailing so with poetry, the greatest difficulties and the fullest ease lie
along known coasts and sounds; there is so much more in the familiar

to work on with the attention, whether conscious or not. The object of these remarks is to suggest why it is appropriate to research, so to speak, the original perils of certain poems of Yeats—those in which one way or another the intellect has wrought life to drama—and thereby to jolt the reader's attention, on as conscious a level as possible, back to those aids to navigation which long practice safely ignores but which alone made the passage, in the beginning, feasible. In this figure it is the intellect, the imagination, the soul that is sailed. The poem is not the ship, the poem is the experience of sailing, the course run, of which it is possible to make certain entries. It should be insisted, though, that these entries in the log only recount and punctuate the voyage, and in no way substitute for it. The experience of sailing cannot be put in any log, in any intellectual record. There is the sea, and there is language, experienced; there is the sailing and the poetry: there are not only no substitutes for these, there is nothing so important as getting back to them unless it be to begin with them.

From 'W. B. Yeats: Between Myth and Philosophy', *Language as Gesture: Essays in Poetry*, London: George Allen and Unwin, 1954, pp. 105–123 (106–109).

DAVID DAICHES

A Recurrent Theme in Yeats's Poetry

I should like now to discuss another theme or attitude (it is sometimes
one and sometimes the other and sometimes both) that can be traced
in the very earliest poems, and which later becomes a distinguishing
quality of much of his greatest poetry. To turn once more to 'The
Sad Shepherd' (not an especially good but nonetheless an interesting
poem): we find in the second line the phrase 'high comrade'
(originally 'high kinsmen'), and we may perhaps say to ourselves that
this use of the adjective 'high' comes from Yeats's preoccupation with
Irish heroic legend and has something to do with the sense of lineage,
of heroic manners, and of exhibitionist courtesy which belongs to such
literature. This is true enough, but there are other things at work here
as well. Here is the first stanza of 'The Rose of the World':

> Who dreamed that beauty passes like a dream?
> For these red lips, with all their mournful pride,
> Mournful that no new wonder may betide,
> Troy passed away in one high funeral gleam,
> And Usna's children died.

This poem dates from 1891. Some nineteen years later, writing of
Maud Gonne in 'No Second Troy', he talked of her beauty as

> Being high and solitary and most stern.

In 'Adam's Curse' (1902), also referring to Maud Gonne, he wrote

> I had a thought for no one's but your ears:
> That you were beautiful, and that I strove
> To love you in the old high way of love; ...

These three examples will suffice. I want to draw attention to the
early stage at which Yeats began to use the word 'high' to indicate
the kind of aristocratic courtesy which he was later to associate with
the life of the Great House, with art patrons of the Italian Renaissance,
with 'innocence and beauty', with 'traditional sanctity and loveliness',
with the tragic gaiety of Hamlet and Lear, and with the horseman who
is enjoined to cast a cold eye on life and on death. There are many
elements compounded here, but they can all be related, however
circuitously, to Yeats's early admiration of the Irish heroic mode. It
is difficult to over-estimate the influence on Yeats of Standish O'Grady's
History of Ireland, Heroic Period (published in 1878). To O'Grady,

wrote Yeats in 1914, 'every Irish imaginative writer owed a portion of his soul'. He went on: 'In his imaginative *History of Ireland* he had made the old Irish heroes, Fion, and Oisin, and Cuchullan, alive again, taking them, for I think he knew no Gaelic, from the dry pages of O'Curry and his school, and condensing and arranging, as he thought Homer would have arranged and condensed. Lady Gregory has told the same tales, . . . but O'Grady was the first, and we read him in our 'teens.'[1] Beside O'Grady's *History* must be set the influence of the character of John O'Leary. 'O'Leary had joined the Fenian movement', wrote Yeats in 1907, 'with no hope of success, as we know, but because he believed such a movement good for the moral character of the people; and had taken his long imprisonment without complaining. Even to the very end, while often speaking of his prison life, he would have thought it took from his Roman courage to describe its hardship. The worth of a man's acts in the moral memory, a continual height of mind in the doing of them, seemed more to him than their immediate result. . . . A man was not to lie, or even to give up his dignity, on any patriotic plea, and I have heard him say, "I have but one religion, the old Persian: to bend the bow and tell the truth", and again, "There are things a man must not do to save a nation", and again "A man must not cry in public to save a nation" . . .'[2] We must bear this passage in mind when we read

> Romantic Ireland's dead and gone,
> It's with O'Leary in the grave,

if we want to be sure that we know what Yeats meant by 'Romantic'.

In the same essay as that in which he described O'Leary's character, Yeats wrote: 'Three types of men have made all beautiful things. Aristocracies have made beautiful manners, because their place in the world puts them above the fear of life, and the countrymen have made beautiful stories and beliefs, because they have nothing to lose and so do not fear, and the artists have made all the rest, because Providence has filled them with recklessness.'[3] Later in this essay he declared that 'in life courtesy and self-possession, and in the arts style, are the sensible impressions of the free mind, for both arise out of a deliberate shaping of all things, and from never being swept away, whatever the emotion, into confusion or dullness'.[4] And one could quote again and again from Yeats's prose writings to show his admiration for traditional courtesy, his belief in the *gesture* (both in life and in art), his view that heroism, sternness, and joy are related in both art and life. 'We will not forget how to be stern, but we will remember always that the highest life unites, as in one fire, the greatest passion and the greatest courtesy.'

---

[1] *The Autobiography of William Butler Yeats*, New York, 1938, pp. 189–90.
[2] *Essays and Introductions*, London, 1961, p. 247.
[3] Op. cit., p. 251.
[4] Op. cit., p. 253.

The 'high funeral gleam' with which Troy passed away is thus an expression of heroic tragedy, of tragedy done with *style*, an idea that from a very early stage possessed Yeats's mind and continued to possess it until the end: we can set the line 'Gaiety transfiguring all that dread' from 'Lapis Lazuli' beside this line from 'The Rose of the World' as representing the final version of this idea. In his early poetry it is related to Irish heroic legend and history, and though later it becomes involved with many other sources this should not lead us to ignore the importance of the Irish elements in this characteristic Yeatsian notion. Yeats's admiration of the Great House tradition, which he came to see as standing for a way of life which converted chaos into order by custom and ceremony, is generally ascribed to the influence on him of Coole Park: but in fact his view of the Irish past had already conditioned him to respond in this way, just as it later helped him to construct his own myth of a great eighteenth-century Anglo-Irish civilization which took in Swift, Berkeley, Sheridan, Goldsmith, Burke and Grattan.

Again and again in Yeats's early poetry we find Irish folklore, Irish heroic story, Irish history and even Irish landscape working in his imagination to mitigate the excesses of self-indulgent romanticism, of mere dreaminess and decorativeness. Long before he knew Pound or became interested in Japanese 'No' plays or came under any of those other influences which strengthened his belief in the importance of stylization in art, he had found Irish reasons for moving in the direction he was to sum up towards the end of his life in the lines beginning

Irish poets, learn your trade,
Sing whatever is well made.

Even the association of classical and Celtic myth in 'The Rose of the World'

Troy passed away in one high funeral gleam,
And Usna's children died—

helps to prevent the image of Helen of Troy from operating as a vague literary reference, concentrating it into a symbol of doomed heroic passion which stands in sharp contrast to the 'cloudy glamour' of other of his early poems. His long-continued hopeless love for Maud Gonne also helped to concentrate his conception of the heroic relationship between beauty, dignity and destruction:

What could have made her peaceful with a mind
That nobleness made simple as a fire,
With beauty like a tightened bow, a kind
That is not natural in an age like this,
Being high and solitary and most stern?
Why, what could she have done, being what she is?
Was there another Troy for her to burn?

These lines come somewhat later. We can see in the earlier poems more clearly the struggle between the vaguely plangent and the stylized heroic. In 'The Rose of Battle' we find:

Rose of all Roses, Rose of all the World!
You, too, have come where the dim tides are hurled
Upon the wharves of sorrow, and heard ring
The bell that calls us on; the sweet far thing.
Beauty grown sad with its eternity
Made you of us, and of the dim grey sea.

This is the early dream style, and adjectives like 'sweet', 'sad', and 'dim' and phrases such as 'the wharves of sorrow' proclaim very plainly to what literary world *this* poem belongs. Sometimes Yeats went over these early poems to change the romantic melancholy into heroic mourning, and the alteration is instructive. Thus the second stanza of 'The Sorrow of Love' originally read:

And when you came with those red mournful lips,
And with you came the whole of the world's tears,
And all the sorrows of her labouring ships,
And all the burden of her myriad years.

This was later changed to

A girl arose that had red mournful lips
And seemed the greatness of the world in tears,
Doomed like Odysseus and the labouring ships
And proud as Priam murdered with his peers; ...

The association of Homeric with Irish themes seems to have done Yeats nothing but good.

From 'Yeats's Earlier Poems: Some Themes and Patterns', *More Literary Essays*, Edinburgh and London: Oliver and Boyd, 1968, pp. 133–49 (143–7). Originally published in A. N. Jeffares and K. G. W. Cross (eds.), *In Excited Reverie: A Centenary Tribute to W. B. Yeats*, London: Macmillan, 1965, pp. 48–67.

Responsibilities

'In dreams begins responsibility.' This quotation, put at the beginning of Yeats's next book of poems, *Responsibilities*, published in 1914, is significant of his change of outlook. The bulk of his early poetry belonged to the dream-world; but that world was essentially irresponsible, implied a reversal or abnegation of the values of the physical world we live in; *The Shadowy Waters* was his last great acclamation of that dream-world. Now the wheel has moved round; the dream-world is taken as a sanction of the world we live in, which latter for Yeats as for Plato is governed by eternal patterns outside itself. Yeats is now shaking free of the concept of transcendence; the relationship between the two worlds is not to be a one-sided one. 'Eternity', he quoted from Blake, 'is in love with the productions of time,' or, in the words of an Irish peasant which he was fond of repeating, 'God possesses the heavens—but he covets the earth.' Our earthly dignity has been vindicated; Yeats is no longer ashamed of our world of conflicting people, of oratory and flesh; he is even beginning to be proud of it as something which may be the disguise of the eternal verities but is also their necessary embodiment. In fighting for a political creed one is following a mythical archetype; in sexual love one is tuning to the music of the spheres.

He was nearly fifty when he published *Responsibilities* and, in the same year, another short narrative poem, *The Two Kings*. The latter is of little interest except that, while it is on the old theme of a woman who is wooed by a supernatural lover, this time the woman is allowed to refuse the lover and make a good case for doing so:

> Never will I believe there is any change
> Can blot out of my memory this life
> Sweetened by death, but if I could believe,
> That were a double hunger in my lips
> For what is doubly brief.

The blank verse of this poem shows little development. It is Victorian blank verse with a fondness for the Swinburnian final anapaest—'More hands in height than any stag in the world.' (for the historian of English blank verse Swinburne would be a significant figure. Since Milton blank verse had been steadily flagging, becoming less alive, more literary. In Tennyson, with his marvellous technical accomplishment, it still retains the aura of a museum. Swinburne, the virtuoso, attempted to galvanize it, applying alliteration and sensual rhythm. *Atalanta in Calydon* is a *tour de force* but the verse fails to be dramatic and its vitality is something factitious.)

Responsibilities, on the other hand, is full of novelties. It is a versatile collection. There are a number of direct personal or occasional poems and some satirical ones. There are examples of a new kind of fable-poetry which avoids becoming allegory. There are a couple of those poems in a ballad form with a refrain which he later was to use so often... these 'ballads' are examples of sleight-of-hand; appearing carefree and frivolous they convey a simple serious statement of a particular mood or idea. Lastly, there are the two poems on 'The Magi' and 'The Dolls', forerunners of his later philosophical poetry.

The fable-poems—'The Grey Rock', 'The Three Beggars', 'The Three Hermits', 'The Hour before Dawn'—are dry, unromantic pieces; an everyday, sometimes colloquial, diction is blended with turns of speech which, though unostentatious, come out of the poetic tradition. 'The Grey Rock' is less interesting for its story rather than for the moral which it points, namely, that a man must keep faith with the eternal powers (the archetypes of art) rather than with any political forces of here and now—'the loud host before the sea'. In an aside Yeats pays a nostalgic tribute to Dowson and Johnson for their single-minded devotion to Art. The story once again presents a supernatural being in love with a man and, in this case, embittered by the man's treachery (a treachery which from another angle is, as in *The Two Kings*, the man's loyalty to his own world):

Why must the lasting love what passes,
Why are the gods by men betrayed?

The poem implies Yeats's peculiar dialectic—eternity in love with the productions of time, the antagonism between gods and men who are divided by a gulf which demands to be bridged so that upon that bridge they can fight or love each other. In different poems Yeats appears to take different sides, an ambiguous partisan because he believes in the final resolution of the rivalry.

'The Three Beggars' is a satirical comment upon everyday avarice; the hero is a crane who, like the fool or the saint elsewhere in his poetry, shows no competitive spirit (the heron for Yeats represents solitude, contemplation). The moral seems to be that quiescence pays in the end:

'Maybe I shall be lucky yet,
Now they are silent,' said the crane.
'Though to my feathers in the wet
I've stood as I were made of stone
And seen the rubbish run about,
It's certain there are trout somewhere

And maybe I shall take a trout
If but I do not seem to care.'

'The Hour before Dawn' points a different moral; it is a defence of the
waking life against the man who intends to sleep till the Day of
Judgment—'For all life longs for the Last Day.' Yeats had in his time
expressed this longing himself and was to continue to express it on
occasions, his allegiance being divided. Now, however, he is on the
whole an accepter of life instead of a rejecter of it; one can see the
influence of Synge:

The beggar in a rage began
Upon his hunkers in the hole,
'It's plain that you are no right man
To mock at everything I love
As if it were not worth the doing.
I'd have a merry life enough
If a good Easter wind were blowing,
And though the winter wind is bad
I should not be too down in the mouth
For anything you did or said
If but this wind were in the south.'

Compare Synge's Tramp in *The Shadow of the Glen*: 'We'll be
going now, I'm telling you, and the time you'll be feeling the cold, and
the frost, and the great rain, and the sun again, and the south wind
blowing in the glens, you'll not be sitting up in a wet ditch, the way
you're after sitting in this place, making yourself old with looking on
each day, and it passing you by. You'll be saying one time, "It's a
good evening, by the grace of God," and another time "It's a wild
night, God help us; but it'll pass surely." '

The same individualist bravado comes out in the magnificent little
poem, 'The Peacock', which begins:

What's riches to him
That has made a great peacock
With the pride of his eye?

and in another poem here that pays homage to a squirrel:

Nor the tame will, nor timid brain,
Nor heavy knitting of the brow
Bred that fierce tooth and cleanly limb
And threw him up to laugh on the bough;
No government appointed him.

Technically, the poems in *Responsibilities* are, for the most part,
very accomplished. Yeats, who composed with extraordinary difficulty,
is outstanding among modern poets for his mastery of the short-line
poem with three or four stresses to a line. Any one who has tried to

write such a poem, when it is not broken into short stanzas, knows
how hard it is so to arrange the sentences as to avoid breaking the
run of the whole, and so to control the rhythms that the poem does not
get into a skid. Yeats, as Mr Oliver St John Gogarty has put it, keeps
his poem balanced in the middle of the page; it does not run off
into the margins. His sentence-construction and rhythmical variation
are structurally functional. Witness the opening lines of a poem from
Responsibilities called 'Friends':

> Now must I these three praise—
> Three women that have wrought
> What joy is in my days:
> One because no thought,
> Nor those unpassing cares,
> No, not in these fifteen
> Many-times-troubled years,
> Could ever come between
> Mind and delighted mind. . . .

It will be noticed here that, though the rhyme scheme is in quatrains,
the chief syntactical stops do not coincide with the ends of the
quatrains. This is a simple mechanical principle, as is the splitting
between one line and the next of epithet and noun or preposition
and noun, but Yeats's craftsmanship is something more than mechanical. He uses many tricks without overdoing any of them. Some intuition guided his half-rhymes, repetitions, counterpointing,[1] his omission
or interpolation of syllables.

The best poems in *Responsibilities* are two short, very direct ones
addressed to Maud Gonne's daughter, which have a Greek and sinewy
spareness. There are more poems for her in his next book and she
ranks among the few persons who could evoke from Yeats this personal
directness. It is incorrrect to say, as some have done, that directness is
the characteristic of Yeats's later poetry or to think that his best
poems are necessarily the direct ones. Much of his later poetry and
some of his finest at that, was oblique, complicated, even obscure.
What we can say is that his later poetry showed a marked increase
in strength and concentration. This strength is sometimes achieved
by directness, sometimes by the powerful girders of ideas, sometimes
by the old enemy rhetoric. Yeats had an epigrammatist in him who
hardly shows himself in his early poetry. As the Celtic mists rolled
away, he was able to look after him and build up his poems more
economically. His material is carefully selected, though he uses the
same properties again and again—the same real life figures, the same
particular events and places, the same stock *personae* and more or less
rigid symbols, the same quasi-philosophical concepts and generaliza-

---

[1] 'Counterpointing': I use Gerard Manley Hopkins's term for the inversion of
the normal metrical stresses; 'Of Man's first disobedience . . .' is counterpointed,
∪ — — ∪ ∪ — ∪ instead of ∪— ∪— ∪— ∪.

tions. The charge of repetition is a favourite weapon of the book-reviewer, a weapon which is often employed stupidly. Provided a concept or a symbol or an image still rings true to a poet, why should he be forbidden to repeat it? It might be pointed out that T. S. Eliot, who has written much less verse, repeats himself frequently both in phrase and image; witness his use of the symbolic figure Coriolanus.

Responsibilities contains two remarkable 'philosophical' poems—'The Magi' and 'The Dolls'—which foreshadow much that is to come in later volumes. Yeats wrote them, as he explains in a note, after having 'noticed once again how all thought among us is frozen into something other than human life'. The dolls, who represent intellectual Being in opposition to physical or physiological Becoming, make an indignant uproar because the doll-maker's wife has had a baby. She, vacillating—like Yeats himself—between the values of life and thought, apologizes to her husband that it was an accident. The Magi in the other poem, 'complementary forms of those enraged dolls', are perceived in the sky with

> all their eyes still fixed, hoping to find once more,
> Being by Calvary's turbulence unsatisfied,
> The uncontrollable mystery on the bestial floor.

As I understand this, it is another view of the dialectic between Being and Becoming. The dolls merely objected to the fact of a human birth. The Magi, being attendants on a birth which is both human and divine, represent the Eternity which is in love with the productions of time but which is repeatedly disappointed by them. Calvary for the Magi is merely a frustration.

Yeats believed—or tried hard to believe—in historical cycles. The birth of Christ therefore, not being a unique phenomenon, was something which must recur. (See his later poem, 'The Second Coming'.) The eternal Powers can only find satisfaction in the dramas played under their own influence or inspiration on the stage of history—as if Plato's Forms could only find themselves in their *mimesis* by particulars. No one point or episode or agent in the drama is satisfying to them; they must have the whole, *the whole of parts*. The defeat of the hero in the play is their defeat because he is their hero but the play as a whole is their triumph because it is their play. So Yeats wrote later in the chorus in *The Resurrection*:

> Odour of blood when Christ was slain
> Made all Platonic tolerance vain
> And vain all Doric Discipline.

The Magi, in so far as they are thought frozen into something other than itself, into Platonized or Doricized transcendentals, were thereby defeated. But, Yeats seems to admit, the Magi themselves are our misrepresentation—ours or Plato's or Lycurgus'—of the supreme spiritual powers. Thought at its highest merges into spirit, Yeats being an idealist who assumes that spirit is the primary and ultimate reality. The descent into time means a splitting of this primary reality into those secondary half-realities opposed to each other whose mutual antagonism implies their mutual dependence. This metaphysical dialectic underlies much of Yeats's later poetry and is involved with his doctrine of reincarnation as well as with that of historical cycles. Neither of these two subsidiary doctrines follows necessarily from the dialectic but Yeats prefers to find them in its manifestations because they enforce the pattern so emphatically.

The discovery that real life is a play and that legend is always in the making encouraged Yeats to jettison his romantic bric-à-brac, to 'hurl helmets, crowns, and swords into the pit'. In *Responsibilities* he abdicates the throne of the twilight:

> I made my song a coat
> Covered with embroideries
> Out of old mythologies
> From heel to throat;
> But the fools caught it,
> Wore it in the world's eyes
> As though they'd wrought it.
> Song, let them take it,
> For there's more enterprise
> In walking naked.

He did not forgo embroideries altogether but from now on they are applied more sparingly and to better advantage.

From *The Poetry of W. B. Yeats,* London: Faber and Faber, 1967, pp. 102–108. (Originally published by Oxford University Press, 1941.)

DANIEL HOFFMAN

Yeats's Use of the Ballad Form

Yeats, as Richard Ellmann observes, turned to the ballad as did Wordsworth, Coleridge and Scott—we might add Burns—partly to purify the diction of verse. Folk ballads were the natural place to seek that diction based on common speech and heightened by passion which Wordsworth had avowed to be the basis of his poems in *Lyrical Ballads*. 'It was a long time before I had made a language to my liking,' Yeats wrote in 1937:

> I began to make it when I discovered some twenty years ago that I must seek, not as Wordsworth thought, words in common use, but a powerful and passionate syntax, and a complete coincidence between period and stanza. Because I need a passionate syntax for passionate subject-matter I compel myself to accept those traditional metres that have developed with the language. . . . I must choose a traditional stanza, even what I alter must seem traditional.'[1]

In his three books after *The Rose* (1893) Yeats seems to have given up ballad-writing, but in *Responsibilities* (1914) he returns to this traditional form. In the meantime he had written his heroic farce, *The Green Helmet* (1910), and chosen as the metre for this play the rhymed fourteeners characteristic of broadside balladry. This crudely forceful metre was admirably adapted to the boisterous energy of that play. Now, returning to the ballad as a lyrical form, he writes in 'Beggar to Beggar Cried' and 'Running to Paradise' with a toughness and a swiftness unanticipated in his earlier efforts. As the second title suggests these do indeed still treat his old theme of flight from necessity, but with a new strength and hardness that makes the attempt itself a part of his desired poetry of insight.

The new note is evident in 'Beggar to Beggar Cried':

> 'Time to put off the world and go somewhere
> And find my health again in the sea air,'
> *Beggar to beggar cried, being frenzy-struck,*
> 'And make my soul before my pate is bare.'
>
> 'And get a comfortable wife and house
> To rid me of the devil in my shoes,'
> *Beggar to beggar cried, being frenzy-struck,*
> 'And the worse devil that is between my thighs.'

---

[1] *Essays and Introductions*, New York, 1961, pp. 523–4.

Three notable innovations: the harsh sensuality; the harsh dissonances of 'house/shoes/thighs'; and the equally harsh refrain, deliberately off-key and displaced to the unexpected third line in the middle of the narrative. Such concentrated dissonance shows how functionally Yeats envisages his form, yet 'even what I alter must seem traditional'.

In this poem Yeats has uncovered the secret of the ballad. Hitherto, although he had written many lyrics with refrains, he had used refrains in hardly any of his ballads.[2] And until now the refrains of his verses had always been merely a reiteration, sometimes in a longer or shorter line than the stanza itself, of the prevailing mood. In 'The Madness of King Goll' the refrain offered after every twelve lines whispered, *They will not hush, the leaves a-flutter round me, the beech leaves old*,' while the refrain to 'Red Hanrahan's Song About Ireland' invokes, in a line as mellifluous as the rest of the song, the name of 'Cathleen, the daughter of Houlihan'. But in the present ballad Yeats has reversed our expectations by making the refrain line discordant and unsingable. From this reversal comes a tonal dialectic between refrain and stanza, between speech and song, a contrast Yeats will develop further in later ballads. This contrast opens the way to a deepening of texture, a richness of meaning, a double movement embedded in sound and rhythm as well as in image.

The argument of 'Beggar to Beggar Cried' projects the beggar's thoughts of marriage and settling down to a respectable life. His perplexity is suggested in the first two lines of the ballad, in which thought of a pilgrimage of the soul is immediately contradicted by the suggestion of a seaside holiday. Shall he make his soul? Shall he 'get a comfortable wife and house'?

> 'And there I'll grow respected at my ease,
> And hear amid the garden's nightly peace,'
> *Beggar to beggar cried, being frenzy-struck,*
> 'The wind-blown clamour of the barnacle-geese.'

The poem tries to objectify Yeats's own dilemma at a time when he suspected 'an unmarried woman past her first youth', with whom he had an anxious liaison, of trying to ensnare him into marriage.[3] By envisaging himself as a beggar he can take on the direct speech and natural syntax of folk expression to universalize his feelings. The beggarman is one of Yeats's favourite devices, indeed becomes one of his masks. Like the Shakespearean fool, the beggar is so unfettered by the claims and bonds of the material world that his simple or daft

---

[2] In the only extended account of Yeats's technique in his ballad poems, Louis Macneice discussed the use of refrains and remarked that the poet achieved 'some of the simplicity or directness or the swing of the primitive form but he does not pretend away (as the early Yeats tried to do) his own sophistication'. *The Poetry of Yeats*, London and New York, 1941, pp. 164-70.

[3] Joseph Hone, *W. B. Yeats, 1865-1939*, New York, 1943, p. 321.

speech reveals ultimate truths and spiritual mysteries. Here, 'being
frenzy-struck', the beggar considers putting aside the wanderings of
his soul for a conventional marriage. But in the last line all the
implications of 'respected at my ease' and 'the garden's nightly peace'
—so inappropriate for a wandering beggar-man—are suddenly reversed
by the heavily accented 'wind-blown clamour of the barnacle-geese'.
Reversed not only metrically but implicitly; the barnacle-goose is a
bird well known in folklore, and there is a belief prevalent in the
West of Ireland that it is hatched from barnacles and therefore is a
fish. Its flesh is eaten on Fridays, hence a symbol of immortality.[4] But
the significance is double. The flight of the geese is doubtless north-
ward, toward the Back of the North Wind, the land of the dead, and
their honking cry is associated with the widespread belief in the Wild
Hunt, the fearful sound of unhallowed souls of the dead, portending
trouble and storm.

The companion ballad takes us also to the Otherworld, but this time
the beggar is 'Running to Paradise':

> As I came over Windy Gap
> They threw a halfpenny into my cap,
> For I am running to Paradise;
> And all that I need do is to wish
> And somebody puts his hand in the dish
> To throw me a bit of salted fish:
> *And there the king is but as the beggar.*

'Perhaps his most consummate triumphs', Edwin Muir wrote of this
poem, 'are in his simple riddling songs, filled with the realistic yet
credulous imagination of the peasantry. That is the kind of song
the peasantry might make if they still made songs, with its shrewd
evaluation of worldly good, and its belief in another world.'[5] Again
the spokesman is a beggar, partaking of fish. 'Windy Gap' is the spot
at which the spirits of the dead would appear to a mortal, and summon
or abduct him. Whether a gap in a wall or a pass between the
mountains, this place of the wind is the 'Steep Gap of the Strangers'
in Yeats's story 'Hanrahan's Vision', and the motif is one he had
himself collected from the peasant folk.[6] The wind contains the whirling dead, the trooping fairies, Herodias' daughters, a vivid image from
folklore which Yeats could enrich with suggestions of dance pattern
and gyre-like movement.

> The wind is old and still at play
> While I must hurry upon my way,

[4] Maria Leach (ed.), *Standard Dictionary of Folklore, Mythology and Legend*,
New York, 1949, I, 460; Charles Swainson, *The Folklore and Provincial Names
of British Birds*, London, 1886, pp. 149–50.
[5] *The Estate of Poetry*, Cambridge, Mass., 1962, p. 58.
[6] *Mythologies*, p. 248; 'The Broken Gates of Death', *Fortnightly Review*,
April 1898, p. 528; 'Irish Witch Doctors', ibid., Sept. 1900, p. 443.

For I am running to Paradise;
Yet never have I lit on a friend
To take my fancy like the wind
That nobody can buy or bind:
And there the king is but as the beggar.

Years later, in 'The Municipal Gallery Revisited', Yeats would write of Synge, himself, and Lady Gregory,

All that we did, all that we said or sang
Must come from contact with the soil, from that
Contact everything Antaeus-like grew strong.
We three alone in modern times had brought
Everything down to that sole test again,
Dream of the noble and the beggar-man.

In Yeats's imagined heroic Ireland, noble and beggarman could put thought and art and act to 'that sole test' because culture was unified and all shared alike in its traditions. In 'Running to Paradise', however, there is the sharp recognition that such a world is transcendent, to be found only in the perfection of death, when '*the king is but as the beggar*'. In this lilting ballad, that is the one line that cannot be sung: reality breaking up the music of the dreaming heart.

From Chapter 2 (' "I am of Ireland": Yeats the Ballad Poet'), D. G. Hoffman, *Barbarous Knowledge: Myth in the Poetry of Yeats, Graves and Muir*, New York: Oxford University Press, 1967, pp. 27–59 (41–6).

FRANK KERMODE

Poetry as Image: *Sailing to Byzantium* and *Among School Children*

I come now, having commented on some of Yeats's other dancers, to the poem in which the Dancer makes her most remarkable appearance. 'Among School Children' is the work of a mind which is itself a system of symbolic correspondences, self-exciting, difficult because the particularities are not shared by the reader—but his interests are not properly in the mind but in the product, which is the sort of poetry that instantly registers itself as of the best. What I have to say of the poem should not be read as an attempt to provide another explication of it, or to provide a psychological contribution to the understanding of the poet. I have, as the preceding pages show, a rather narrow interest in its images, and that is what I propose to pursue.

The 'sixty-year-old smiling public man' of the poem is caught in the act of approving, because he has ventured out of his *genre*, of a way of educating children which, as we have seen, is completely inimical to his profoundest convictions. The tone is of self-mockery, gentle and indeed somewhat mincing, with a hint of unambitious irony—'in the best modern way', we can pick up this note without prior informa- tion, but it is at any rate interesting to know that the children are engaged in the wrong labour, the antithesis of the heroic labour of the looking-glass. The old man, because he is old and a *public* man, does not protest, but sees himself as amusingly humiliated, not too seriously betrayed, putting up with the shapelessness and common- ness that life has visited upon him. But children of the kind he sees before him remind him of the great image of a lady who was all they could not hope to be, a daughter of imagination, not of memory; a daughter of the swan, the perfect emblem of the soul, and like Leda the sign of an annunciation of paganism and heroic poetry, for which the soul is well-lost. But she too is old; he thinks of her present image: 'Did Quattrocento finger fashion it?' For even in old age she has that quality of the speaking body, the intransigent vision, perhaps, of Mantegna. And he himself had had beauty, though he had spent it in his isolation and intellectual effort, and become shapeless and common, the old scarecrow of the later poems. The fifth stanza develops this theme, the destruction of the body by Adam's curse,

which for Yeats is the curse of labour. It is a reworking of some lines
from 'At The Hawk's Well", of ten years earlier.

> A mother that saw her son
> Doubled over with speckled shin,
> Cross-grained with ninety years,
> Would cry, 'How little worth
> Were all my hopes and fears
> And the hard pain of his birth!'

This old man has lain in wait for fifty years, but he 'is one whom the
dancers cheat'; 'wisdom', conclude the singers, 'must lead a bitter life',
and he who pursues it prizes the dry stones of a well and the leafless
tree above a comfortable door and an old hearth, children and the
indolent meadows. This is the plight of the old man in the schoolroom,
to be with the scarecrow thinkers and teachers and poets, out of life;
the scarecrow is the emblem of such a man, because he is an absurd,
rigid diagram of living flesh that would break the heart of the woman
who suffered the pang of his birth.

But there are other heartbreakers, though these do not change with
time, but 'keep a marble or a bronze repose'. 'Marble and bronze' is a
recurrent minor motive in Yeats. It occurs in simple form in 'The
Living Beauty' (1919), where there is an antithetical relationship
between it and that which is truly 'alive'—alive in the normal sense,
and possessing that speaking body which includes the soul.

> I bade, because the wick and oil are spent,
> And frozen are the channels of the blood,
> My discontented heart to draw content
> From beauty that is cast out of a mould
> In bronze, or that in dazzling marble appears,
> Appears, but when we have gone is gone again,
> Being more indifferent to our solitude
> Than 'twere an apparition. O heart, we are old;
> The living beauty is for younger men:
> We cannot pay its tribute of wild tears.

These masterly verses have the seeds of much later poetry. The
purpose of art, in the life of the poet, is to mitigate isolation by
providing the Image which is the daily victory. 'I suffered continual
remorse, and only became content when my abstractions had composed
themselves into picture and dramatization . . .' But the relief is
impermanent; the poet discovers that 'he has made, after the manner
of his kind, Mere images'. There is a tormenting contrast between
the images (signified by the bronze and marble statuettes) and the
living beauty. And out of this contrast grows the need for a poetic
image which will resemble the living beauty rather than the marble
or bronze. No static image will now serve; there must be movement,
the different sort of life that a dancer has by comparison with the

most perfect object of art. Here we see, in strictly poetic terms, a change comparable to that wrought by Pound in the abandonment of Imagism, and the development of a dynamic image-theory. The Image is to be all movement, yet with a kind of stillness. She lacks separable intellectual content, her meanings, as the intellect receives them, must constantly be changing. She has the impassive, characterless face of Salome, so that there is nothing but the dance, and she and the dance are inconceivable apart, indivisible as body and soul, meaning and form, ought to be. The Dancer in fact is, in Yeats's favourite expression, 'self-begotten', independent of labour; as such she differs totally from the artist who seeks her. She can exist only in the pre-destined dancing-place where, free from Adam's curse, beauty is born of itself, without the labour of childbirth or the labour of art; where art means wholly what it *is*. The tree also means what it is, and its beauty is a function of its whole being, achieved without cost, causing no ugliness in an artist. This is one of the senses of the magnificent concluding stanza:

Labour is blossoming or dancing where
The body is not bruised to pleasure soul,
Nor beauty born out of its own despair,
Nor blear-eyed wisdom out of midnight oil.
O chestnut tree, great-rooted blossomer,
Are you the leaf, the blossom or the bole?
O body swayed to music, O brightening glance,
How can we know the dancer from the dance?

'A savoir que la danseuse *n'est pas une femme qui danse,* pour ces motifs juxtaposés qu'elle *n'est pas une femme,* mais une méta-phore résumant un des aspects élémentaires de notre forme, glaive, coupe, fleur, etc., et *qu'elle ne danse pas,* suggérant, par le prodige de raccourcis ou d'élans, avec une écriture corporelle ce qu'il faudrait des paragraphes en prose dialoguée autant que descriptive, pour exprimer, dans la rédaction: *poèm dégagé de tout appareil du scribe.*'

This is Mallarmé's accurate prediction of Yeats's poem.

'Among School Children' might well be treated as the central state-ment of the whole complex position of isolation and the Image. Later there were many fine poems that dealt with the nature of the sacrifice, and of the fugitive victory; like 'Vacillation', which asks the question 'What is joy?' and answers it with an image, of a sort to be achieved only by choosing the way of Homer and shunning salvation; or like the 'Dialogue of Self and Soul', or the simple statement of 'The Choice':

The intellect of man is forced to choose
Perfection of the life or of the work,
And if it choose the second must refuse

A heavenly mansion, raging in the dark.

When all the story's finished, what's the news?
In luck or out the toil has left its mark:
That old perplexity an empty purse,
Or the day's vanity, the night's remorse.

There are poems, too, which give the problem a more specifically religious turn. The paradise in which labour and beauty are one, where beauty is self-begotten and costs nothing, is the artificial paradise of a poet deeply disturbed by the cost of labour. The ambiguities of hatred and love for 'marble and bronze' inform not only those poems in which Yeats praises the active aristocratic life and its courtesies, but also the Byzantium poems, which also celebrate the paradisal end of the dilemma. In this paradise life, all those delighting manifestations of growth and change in which the scarecrow has forfeited his part, give way to a new condition in which marble and bronze are the true life and inhabit a changeless world, beyond time and intellect (become, indeed, the image truly conceived, without human considerations of cost). The artist himself may be imagined, therefore, a changeless thing of beauty, purged of shapelessness and commonness induced by labour, himself a self-begotten and self-delighting marble or bronze. 'It is even possible that being is only possessed completely by the dead'; we return to the ambiguous life or death of the Image. Those who generate and die, perpetually imperfect in their world of becoming, have praise only for that world; the old man has no part in it, praising only the withered tree and the dry well, hoping only for escape into the world of complete being, the world of the self-begotten. 'The artifice of eternity', like 'the body of this death', is a reversible term.

'Sailing to Byzantium' could scarcely be regarded as less than a profoundly considered poem; yet Yeats was willing to accept the criticism of the acute Sturge Moore that the antithesis of the birds of the dying generations and the golden bird was imperfect; and this consideration was one of the causes of the second poem, 'Byzantium'. 'Your "Sailing to Byzantium"', wrote Moore, 'magnificent as the first three stanzas are, lets me down in the fourth, as such a goldsmith's bird is as much nature as man's body, especially if it only sings like Homer and Shakespeare of what is past or passing or to come to Lords and Ladies.' Yeats sent him a copy of 'Byzantium' so that he should have an idea of what was needed for the symbolic cover design of his new book (at this time he was going to call it not *The Winding Stair* but *Byzantium*) and added that Moore's criticism was the origin of the new poem—it had shown the poet that 'the idea needed exposition'. Only a little earlier, by the way, Moore had provided Yeats with a copy of Flecker's 'A Queen's Song', which has a certain relevance to 'Byzantium', being a treatment of the topic of living beauty *versus* bronze and marble, or in this instance, gold:

Had I the power
To Midas given of old
To touch a flower
And leave its petal gold
I then might touch thy face,
Delightful boy,
And leave a metal grace
A graven joy.

Thus would I slay—
Ah! desperate device!—
The vital day
That trembles in thine eyes,
And let the red lips close
Which sang so well
And drive away the rose
To leave a shell.

We have already seen why Yeats was so interested in Byzantine art; it gave him that sense of an image totally estranged from specifically human considerations (and particularly from discursive intellect) with meaning and form identical, the vessel of the spectator's passion, which led him to develop the Dancer image. These lines of Flecker point also towards that life-in-death, death-in-life, which characterizes the perfect being of art. The absolute difference, as of different orders of reality, between the Image and what is, in the usual sense, alive, was the crucial point upon which the first Byzantium poem had, on Moore's view, failed; it was so important to the poet that he did his work again, making the distinction more absolute, seeking some more perfect image to convey the quality, out of nature and life and becoming, of the apotheosized marble and bronze. The bird must absolutely be a bird of artifice; the entire force of the poem for Yeats depended upon this—otherwise he would scarcely have bothered about Moore's characteristic, and of course intelligent, quibble. Professor N. Jeffares has shown how full are the opening lines of 'Sailing to Byzantium' of peculiarly powerful suggestions of natural life, the life of generation; the salmon carries obvious suggestions of sexual vigour, and, it might be added, of that achieved physical beauty Yeats so much admired, immense power and utter singleness of purpose, in the business of generating and dying. Of course the golden bird must be the antithesis of this, as well as the heavenly counterpart of old scarecrows. It prophesies, speaks out as the foolish and passionate need not; it uses the language of courtesy in a world where all the nature-enforced discriminations of spirit and body, life and death, being and becoming, are meaningless. 'Marbles of the dancing floor/Break bitter furies of complexity.' And it is this world that Byzantium symbolizes. Mr Jeffares says the bird is different in the second poem because 'here it is explicitly contrasted with natural birds, to their disadvantage'.

In fact the same contrast is intended in the earlier poem; the new degree of explicitness is what Moore's criticism forced upon the poet. The focus of attention is no longer on the poignancy of the contrast between nature and art in these special senses; nature now becomes 'mere complexities, The fury and the mire,' and the strategy of the poem is, clearly, to establish the immense paradoxical vitality of the dead, more alive than the living; still, but richer in movement than the endless agitation of becoming.

And this is precisely the concept of the dead face and the dancer, the mind moving like a top, which I am calling the central icon of Yeats and of the whole tradition. Byzantium is where this is the normal condition, where all is image and there are no contrasts and no costs, inevitable concomitants of the apparition of absolute being in the sphere of becoming. We can harm the poem by too exclusive an attention to its eschatology, and it is salutary to read it simply as a marvellously contrived emblem of what Yeats took the work of art to be. There is no essential contradiction between the readings. The reconciling force is Imagination, the creator of the symbol by which men 'dream and so create Translunar Paradise'. Or, to use the completely appropriate language of Blake, 'This world of Imagination is the world of Eternity; it is the divine bosom into which we shall all go after the death of the Vegetated body. This World of Imagination is Infinite & Eternal, whereas the world of Generation, or Vegetation, is Finite & Temporal ... The Human Imagination ... appear'd to Me ... throwing off the Temporal that the Eternal might be Establish'd ... In Eternity one Thing never Changes into another Thing. Each Identity is Eternal.' There is no better gloss on Yeats's poem, a poem impossible outside the tradition of the Romantic Image and its corollary, the doctrine of necessary isolation and suffering in the artist.

In poems later than these, Yeats continues the search for the reconciling image; and he constantly recurs to the theme of remorse, the lost perfection of the life. His 'Dejection Ode', at last, is 'The Circus Animal's Desertion'. The poet sought a theme, without finding one:

Maybe at last, being but a broken man,
I must be satisfied with my heart ...

The 'heart' is the self, speaking out stilled fury and lifeless mire; it is that which has been denied for the work. He enumerates the old themes which had served in the past to cheat the heart, and presents them all, unfairly bitter, as the consolations merely of his own imperfection and estrangement. Oisin was sent through the islands of 'vain gaiety, vain battle, vain repose' to satisfy an amorous need in the poet; *The Countess Cathleen* had its origin in a private fear for a mistress, but soon enough

This dream itself had all my thought and love.

And this was the way with all his themes.

And when the Fool and Blind Man stole the bread
Cuchulain fought the ungovernable sea;
Heart-mysteries there, and yet when all is said
It was the dream itself enchanted me:
Character isolated by a deed
To engross the present and dominate memory.
Players and painted stage took all my love,
And not those things that they were emblems of.

'Players and painted stage' are here the dream, the work of imagination which relegates 'real' life to a position of minor importance. Hence
the final stanza; like the fresh images of Byzantium, these images begin
in fury and mire, among the dying generations, and are changed in the
dream of imagination. When this no longer works, the poet falls back
into the 'formless spawning fury', left to live merely, when living is
most difficult, life having been used up in another cause.

Those masterful images because complete
Grew in pure mind, but out of what began?
A mound of refuse or the sweepings of a street,
Old kettles, old bottles, and a broken can,
Old iron, old bones, old rags, that raving slut
That keeps the till. Now that my ladder's gone,
I must lie down where all the ladders start,
In the foul rag-and-bone shop of the heart.

The increasingly autobiographical quality of the later poems is justified precisely by this need to examine the relation of process to
product, of dying generations to bronze and marble. We are
reminded of the extraordinary proportion of biographical matter in
Coleridge's poem, particularly in the first version of it. If we wanted to
study Yeats as hero, we could dwell upon the astonishing pertinacity
with which he faced, and the integrity with which he solved, a
problem which can never be far from the surface of poetry in this
tradition; the Image is always likely to be withdrawn, indeed almost
any normal biographical situation is likely to cause its withdrawal—
this is part of its cost. Coleridge was finished as a poet in his early
thirties; Arnold's situation is in this respect rather similar. Yeats often
faced the crisis; the Autobiographies show how often, and how
desperately, and many poems are made out of it. When poetry is
Image, life must, as Yeats said, be tragic.
   The dead face which has another kind of life, distinct from that
human life associated with intellectual activity; the dancer, insepar-
able from her dance, devoid of expression—that human activity which
interferes with the Image—turning, with a movement beyond that of
life, in her narrow luminous circle and costing everything; the bronze
and marble that do not provide the satisfactions of the living beauty
but represent a higher order of truth, of being as against becoming,

which is dead only in that it cannot change: these are the images of the Image that I have considered in this chapter. They culminate, in Yeats, in the Dancer-image of 'Among School Children'; and so does the image of the Tree. This image summarizes the traditional Romantic critical analogy of art as organism. . . .

From Chapter IV ('The Dancer'), *Romantic Image*, London: Routledge and Kegan Paul, 1957, pp. 49–91 (82–91).

THOMAS R. WHITAKER

Meditations in Time of Civil War

The poem ['Introductory Rhymes' to *Responsibilities*] measures both
the speaker's limitation—his failure to maintain the solid virtues and
to transmit yet further his inherited stamina—and his acceptance of
that limitation. For his 'barren passion' is itself a 'wasteful virtue' and
a result of the 'die's cast'. Even his wastefulness has a peculiar
solidity: the deprecated 'book' makes articulate the hitherto silent
gestures of soldier and skipper and even the undefined 'daily spectacle'
of the fierce old man. It transmits within its own half-legendary world
the qualities that seem (since the beginning of the 'story') always to
have belonged to such a world. In the restraint, irony, and well-
grounded pride of his apology, as in the breadth of his admirations,
the speaker himself thus incarnates the inheritance that he addresses.
   If this is a mere 'book', it is one which mirrors life with a strange
fullness. In fact, these lines set the stage for a dramatic interplay
throughout *Responsibilities* between 'book' and 'child', 'doll' and
'baby', 'art' and 'life'. Every poem must resolve that tension, often
through explicit discussion of the tension itself, and so become a
more complete art than the 'book' it deprecates or the 'priceless things'
it wryly defends—an art of living images. The creation of such
images, of course, has begun long before the actual 'composition' of
poems. Yeats wrote of William Pollexfen: 'Even today when I read
King Lear his image is always before me and I often wonder if the
delight in passionate men in my plays and in my poetry is more than
his memory.'[1] It *was* more, as the prologue to *Responsibilities*
suggests: for the memory itself is partly a function of that delight—
partly a shadow cast by the passionate self of the poet. The speaker
mirrors his inheritance partly because that inheritance, as he sees it,
has emerged in consciousness as a complex image of his state. The
poems can so richly reconcile life and art because they arise in a mind
that views history as a realm of 'interchange among streams or
shadows', where 'one could never say which was man and which was
shadow'—a realm of shades more than men, more images than shades,
where discovery and creation, receiving and giving, are inextricably
mingled.

ii

The dialogue between self and shadows—whether antiselves or projec-

[1] *Autobiographies*, p. 5.

tions of the self—produced in 'Meditations in Time of Civil War' a rich orchestration of personal and historical conflicts. The poem is a complex act of creation and self-judgment in the realm of the spiritualized soil.

'Surely . . .' The dialogue enters with that stress on the very first word, as the speaker yearningly considers 'Ancestral Houses'. Already the opening sentence contains the seeds of its own negation:

> Surely among a rich man's flowering lawns,
> Amid the rustle of his planted hills,
> Life overflows without ambitious pains . . .

Gradually the image of the fountain emerges, establishing the correspondence of spirit and soil which underlies the entire poem. But the pale abstractness of the setting, in which the fountain alone 'rains down life', already calls into question the reality of that social ideal. The retort is deserved: 'Mere dreams, mere dreams!' But a surprising counterassertion follows:

> Yet Homer had not sung
> Had he not found it certain beyond dreams
> That out of life's own self-delight had sprung
> The abounding glittering jet . . .

It is the intuition of a radical self-sufficiency and vitality, which has been too hastily projected into the inadequate landscape of ancestral houses. The allusion to Homer suggests the reason for the inadequacy: sweetness must come from strength. Life cannot merely overflow 'without ambitious pains'; the 'abounding glittering jet' results from a pent-up force that can surmount obstacles. The dream must be revised: it is precisely the ambitious pains of violent and bitter men that

> might rear in stone
> The sweetness that all longed for night and day,
> The gentleness none there had ever known . . .

Instead of an effortless fountain, a monumental synthesis of opposites: but though 'in stone', such a synthesis is momentary, a historical climax which bears the seeds of its own destruction. The eighteenth-century elegance, mimed in the verse itself, renders ambitious pains unnecessary and dries up the fountain:

> O what if levelled lawns and gravelled ways
> Where slippered Contemplation finds his ease
> And Childhood a delight for every sense,
> But take our greatness with our violence?

Where then may the speaker himself seek the transfiguration of the fallen world? He turns from the world dreamed of to the world possessed, from 'Ancestral Houses' to 'My House'. At the time he was writing this sequence, in 1921–22, Yeats was relating the 'sense of possession' he had felt in Sligo to his concept of 'Unity of Being':

> 'All that moves us is related to our possible Unity; we lose interest in the abstract and concrete alike; only when we have said, 'My fire', and so distinguished it from 'the fire' and 'a fire', does the fire seem bright. Every emotion begins to be related, as musical notes are related, to every other.'[2]

In 'My House' we see a measure of historical continuity, but also strength and even violence:

> An ancient bridge, and a more ancient tower,
> A farmhouse that is sheltered by its wall,
> An acre of stony ground,
> Where the symbolic rose can break in flower,
> Old ragged elms, old thorns innumerable,
> The sound of the rain or sound
> Of every wind that blows . . .

Isaiah had prophesied the spiritualization of a soil very like this stony ground: 'The wilderness and the solitary place shall be glad for them; and the desert shall rejoice, and blossom as the rose.' Blake had envisioned in such a place the marriage of Heaven and Hell:

> Roses are planted where thorns grow,
> And on the barren heath
> Sing the honey bees[3]

But in the harsh Yeatsian landscape even the symbolic rose must *break* in flower.

Here the speaker does not inherit the glory of the rich; he re-enacts the founding of a house:

> Two men have founded here. A man-at-arms
> Gathered a score of horse and spent his days
> In this tumultuous spot,
> Where through long wars and sudden night alarms
> His dwindling score and he seemed castaways
> Forgetting and forgot;
> And I, that after me
> My bodily heirs may find
> To exalt a lonely mind,
> Befitting emblems of adversity.

The isolated modern poet's need to forge his own tradition may itself be a condition of great achievement: his spiritual inheritance is that of adversity, with its attendant opportunities. Yet the comparison of founders ominously reduces the man-at-arms to the speaker's own

---

[2] *A Vision* (1925), p. 61.
[3] Isaiah 35:1; Blake, *Complete Writings*, p. 148.

proud and introverted isolation. Such was not the condition of those violent, bitter men who could rear in stone the sweetness and gentleness that all had longed for. In a wilderness where art is divorced from power and communion, the symbolic rose threatens to be more dream than reality.

That lurking conflict is already evident in the first stanza of 'My House'. This is a poem of interior landscapes, one in which 'familiar woods and rivers . . . fade into symbol'. The speaker might say with Wordsworth,

> bodily eyes
> Were utterly forgotten, and what I saw
> Appeared like something in myself, a dream,
> A prospect in the mind

—or feel with Coleridge that the object of Nature is 'the dim awaking of a forgotten or hidden truth of my inner nature'.[4] Hence, as we move from 'Old ragged elms, old thorns innumerable', to

> The stilted water-hen
> Crossing stream again
> Scared by the splashing of a dozen cows . . .

we should suspect an ironic self-image, as yet unexplored. The second stanza takes up that stilted isolation, presenting as another spiritual ancestor Milton's Platonist, atop his winding stair, in his 'chamber arched with stone', withdrawn from the crude traffic of the world:

> Benighted travellers
> From markets and from fairs
> Have seen his midnight candle glimmering.

The ironic parallels are as yet but implicit; the speaker has not allowed himself to examine his proud isolation in full daylight.

Asking why such blindness is possible, we note a further implication in the Platonist who, the speaker imagines,

> toiled on
> In some like chamber, shadowing forth
> How the daemonic rage
> Imagined everything.

Both he and his spiritual heir, though lonely creators of emblems, castaways from the world of markets and fairs, are yet at home in a lighted chamber, communing with the world soul, while others are 'benighted'. But they do not commune with the 'holy calm' that overspread Wordsworth's soul and caused him to see the landscape as a prospect in the mind. The demiurgic power as this speaker exper-

---

[4] William Wordsworth, *The Prelude*, Bk. 2, lines 349ff.; Samuel Taylor Coleridge, *Anima Poetae*, Boston, 1895, p. 115.

iences it is a 'daemonic rage', the transcendental corollary of his own
bitter violence and of the 'long wars and sudden night alarms' that
isolate him as they once isolated the first founder in this spot. Again
the poem's complex theme modulates from reassuring unity to division
and fragmentation. But the conflicts in 'My House' are submerged,
apparent only because the speaker is shadowing forth more complete
emblems of his own condition than he yet admits.

He turns now to another possession, the table whereon he shadows
forth that daemonic rage. Into his world of adversity, isolation and
cyclical change comes 'Sato's gift, a changeless sword', placed by
pen and paper

> That it may moralize
> My days out of their aimlessness.

But for a poet aware of the virtues of change as well as its dangers,
that is a vexing symbol:

> In Sato's house,
> Curved like new moon, moon-luminous,
> It lay five hundred years.
> Yet if no change appears
> No moon; only an aching heart
> Conceives a changeless work of art.

Though a world of tortured change needs an image of the changeless,
does not that image itself imply a fallacious ideal, a static culture,
empty and unproductive?[5] No, the speaker surmounts his objection
by imagining in the East an unchanging tradition maintained by
centuries of mental alertness, inspired by transcendental longings:

> Soul's beauty being most adored,
> Men and their business took
> The soul's unchanging look;
> For the most rich inheritor,
> Knowing that none could pass Heaven's door
> That loved inferior art,
> Had such an aching heart
> That he, although a country's talk
> For silken clothes and stately walk,
> Had walking wits; it seemed
> Juno's peacock screamed.

There, in contrast to the milieu of 'Ancestral Houses', the grandson
was no 'mouse', the 'inherited glory of the rich' was not an empty
shell, the peacock did not merely stray 'with delicate feet upon old
terraces' while Juno was ignored by the 'garden deities'.

---

[5] For an earlier description of Eastern traditionalism ('the painting of Japan,
not having our European Moon to churn its wits . . .') see *Essays and Introductions*
(1916), p. 225.

But is that peacock scream, that apocalyptic annunciation,[6] more than another illusion? Whether dream or past reality—and it is slightly distanced by the ironic diction of this section—it can now do no more than stimulate this speaker's aching heart. Is that not function enough? An ambiguous answer emerges in the next section, 'My Descendants'. Returning to the cyclical world of the West, to the lunar inheritance which for better or worse he must enjoy and transmit, the speaker presents himself as one who 'must nourish dreams'—but is he obligated or condemned to do so? And are they unsubstantial fantasies or symbolic roses, evasion or transfiguration of life?

> Having inherited a vigorous mind
> From my old fathers, I must nourish dreams
> And leave a woman and a man behind
> As vigorous of mind, and yet it seems
> Life scarce can cast a fragrance on the wind,
> Scarce spread a glory to the morning beams,
> But the torn petals strew the garden plot;
> And there's but common greenness after that.

But if his descendants should lose that ambiguous flower, he would, enraged, hasten the very cyclical destruction that haunts him:

> May this laborious stair and this stark tower
> Become a roofless ruin that the owl
> May build in the cracked masonry and cry
> Her desolation to the desolate sky.

No longer dare he hope that his 'bodily heirs' may find, to their advantage, 'Befitting emblems of adversity'. He may be both founder and last inheritor—

> The Primum Mobile that fashioned us
> Has made the very owls in circles move

—and he will therefore take consolation only in the goods of the moment:

> And I, that count myself most prosperous,
> Seeing that love and friendship are enough,
> For an old neighbour's friendship chose the house
> And decked and altered it for a girl's love . . .

Though still unable to refrain from adding another phrase which contemplates at least some bare monument to the present—

> And know whatever flourish and decline
> These stones remain their monument and mine

—in his minimal optimism he has now abandoned even the immortal-

[6] *A Vision* (1937), p. 268.

ity of the 'changeless work of art'. Surely here at least the speaker
may find the self-sufficiency for which he longs: no mere dream, but
the reality of 'life's own self-delight'.

Yet in glimpsing the depths of his isolation, he has begun to reach
outward: 'Seeing that love and friendship are enough'. That evocation of a sweetness and gentleness not 'in stone', as in ancestral
houses, but memorialized by these 'stones', translates the entire problem to a different plane. The isolation itself called into question, the
speaker turns from house and descendants to 'The Road at My Door'.

> An affable Irregular,
> A heavily-built Falstaffian man,
> Comes cracking jokes of civil war
> As though to die by gunshot were
> The finest play under the sun.

He turns from lunar tragedy to solar comedy, from lofty poetic isolation
to the gay *camaraderie* of a modern man-at-arms—or (in terms of what
Yeats called Shakespeare's dominant myth, and was one of his own)
from that porcelain vessel, Richard II, saluting his native soil with
ostentatious sentiment and telling sad stories of the death of kings,
to those vessels of clay, Falstaff and Prince Hal, with their rough
humour and affection.[7] Adversity and violence need not imply isolation, nor can the poet dismiss this comedy as trivial:

> A brown Lieutenant and his men,
> Half dressed in national uniform,
> Stand at my door, and I complain
> Of the foul weather, hail and rain,
> A pear tree broken by the storm.

It is not a symbolic rose that has broken, and the contrast of persons
recalls the unacknowledged difference in 'My House' between the
introverted speaker and the first founder in that tumultuous spot.
By night the Platonist in his tower had seemed romantically superior
to the travellers; by day the retiring and complaining poet becomes
a half-comic, half-pathetic pastoral foil to the new military hero.[8]

[7] See *Essays and Introductions* (1901), pp. 103–9. There, as in this poem,
Yeats has an eye for the tragic ironies in both porcelain and clay. A simpler use
of the metaphor appeared in *The Countess Cathleen, Collected Poems*, p. 29.

[8] Yeats's use of such a foil comes, of course, from literary tradition as well as
from personal experience. He used it more simply for romantic pathos in *The
Countess Cathleen*, as Cathleen says of the gardener (*Poems*, London, 1895, p. 98):
> Pruning time,
> And the slow ripening of his pears and apples,
> For him is a long, heart-moving history.

In *L'Otage* (p. 14), amidst the breaking of nations, occurs this dialogue:
> Coufontaine: Il était temps de nous mettre a l'abri.
> Je reconnais le vent de mon pays.
> Sygne: Quel dommage! Les pommiers étaient si beaux!
> Il ne restera pas un pépin sur l'arbre.

He is, in fact, like that 'shadow' noted earlier, the stilted waterhen 'Scared by the splashing of a dozen cows'.

> I count those feathered balls of soot
> The moor-hen guides upon the stream,
> To silence the envy in my thought;
> And turn towards my chamber, caught
> In the cold snows of a dream.

What dream has been nourished? In this solitary place what narcissus has broken in flower? The implied answer is developed in 'The Stare's Nest at My Window,' and it will lead, in 'I See Phantoms . . .', beyond the humility of perception to a new reconciliation: an ironic acceptance of the poet's vocation.

> The bees build in the crevices
> Of loosening masonry, and there
> The mother birds bring grubs and flies.
> My wall is loosening; honey-bees,
> Come build in the empty house of the stare.

He no longer imagines a sweetness that bitter men might rear in stone, nor does he hope defiantly for the destruction of his tower and for owls to 'build in the cracked masonry'. He now sees that sweetness may reside in the very loss he had feared—the very loosening of his wall. This is an inevitable discovery—or rather, rediscovery, for the breaking of protective walls, the nakedness before the winds of heaven, had long been known to Yeats as a prerequisite of poetic vision. Although the invoked honeybees recall those in Porphyry's cave of the nymphs—souls who are 'eminently just and sober' and who, 'after having performed such things as are acceptable to the gods', will reascend from the world of generation[9]—they also, and perhaps more importantly, recall those which Blake imagined as singing on the barren heath, on the desert that blossoms as the rose. Yeats had once read that prophecy thus: 'Freedom shows beauty like roses, and sweetness like that given by the honey of bees, in the road where morality had only revealed a desert or a heath.'[10] Given Blake's understanding of negative and restrictive morality (a disguise for the impulse to tyrannize, to wall others in or out), the sweetness which comes with the abandonment of such morality is not opposed to that ('both cathartic and preservative'[11]) produced by Porphyry's bees. For the speaker of this poem such sweetness can come only with freedom from his own self-confinement. Though able, in Shelley's symbolic language, to imagine his tower as contrary in meaning to a

---

[9] Quoted in *Essays and Introductions* (1900), p. 84; see *Selected Works of Porphyry*, tr. Thomas Taylor, London, 1823, p. 185.

[10] *Essays and Introductions*, p. 61.

[11] *Selected Works of Porphyry*, p. 181.

dark cave,[12] he now sees that the cloistered permanence of his 'chamber arched with stone' is what it always was, the cavern of the mind of which Blake had written: 'For man has closed himself up, till he sees all things thro' narrow chinks of his cavern.'[13] As this speaker states it, now fusing visions of himself and of society:

> We are closed in, and the key is turned
> On our uncertainty; somewhere
> A man is killed, or a house burned,
> Yet no clear fact to be discerned:
> Come build in the empty house of the stare.

He shares Eliot's waste land—

> We think of the key, each in his prison
> Thinking of the key, each confirms a prison
> Only at nightfall, aethereal rumours
> Revive for a moment a broken Coriolanus

—and the waste land of Claudel's Coufontaine:

> Là-bas on dit qu'il y a eu je sais quoi,
> Les villes de bois qui brûlent, une victoire vaguement
> gagnée. L'Europe est vide et personne ne parle sur la terre.[14]

But the besieged dynastic house or prison is not, from this speaker's humbled position, the abbey of Coufontaine or even 'some marvellous empty sea-shell'; it is an empty starling's nest.

Not through coincidence or mere rhetorical artifice does he fuse here the isolation and vastation sprung from his own mind and those imposed by violence from without. He has moved from a romantic parallel between poet and man-at-arms to a humiliating acknowledgment of their differences, and now to an agonized perception of their moral identity:

> A barricade of stone or of wood;
> Some fourteen days of civil war;
> Last night they trundled down the road
> That dead young soldier in his blood:
> Come build in the empty house of the stare.

> We have fed the heart on fantasies,
> The heart's grown brutal from the fare;
> More substance in our enmities
> Than in our love: O honey-bees,
> Come build in the empty house of the stare.

The poet's barricade of self-sufficiency and his consequent self-

---

[12] See Essays and Introductions (1900), p. 87.
[13] Blake, Complete Writings, p. 154.
[14] Claudel, L'Otage, p. 54.

brutalization are, in his introverted realm, equivalent to the nationalist-inspired civil war that rages about him. 'Was not a nation ... bound together by this interchange among streams or shadows ...?' His fantasies that bitterness and violence might bring sweetness, his glorying in adversity, and his rage against his descendants have earned his indictment. But the indictment itself is a partial release from the prison: hence the initial statement, in the first person singular, 'My wall is loosening', leads to community in isolation, 'We are closed in', and then to a perception of shared guilt, a moral identification of self and those beyond all barricades, 'We had fed the heart on fantasies...' In the final cry to the honeybees the arrogant dream of self-sufficiency is transcended; the perception that 'love and friendship are enough' has flowered, purged of its complacency.

The poet can now climb his winding stair, not to a chamber arched with stone, but to the top of a *broken* tower, where he is possessed by a vision:

I climb to the tower-top and lean upon broken stone,
A mist that is like blown snow is sweeping over all,
Valley, river, and elms, under the light of a moon
That seems unlike itself, that seems unchangeable,
A glittering sword out of the east. A puff of wind
And those white glimmering fragments of the mist sweep by.
Frenzies bewilder, reveries perturb the mind;
Monstrous familiar images swim to the mind's eye.

Every 'Space that a Man views around his dwelling-place/Standing on his own roof ... is his Universe'. But as the animating wind makes clear, this universe is no longer a confining mental chamber. The speaker is naked to the winds of heaven. He leans upon the very ruin of self-sufficiency; sweeping over the landscape are the 'cold snows of a dream' shared by those beyond the broken barricades. Though he sees by a light whose ominously unchangeable source is a bizarre transmutation of his own earlier ideal, 'A glittering sword out of the east', and though the 'monstrous' images that come are also damningly 'familiar', this is no private fantasy but a vision based upon his own complicity in the engulfing horror.

The first group of phantoms objectifies the brutality and hatred he has just recognized:

'Vengeance upon the murderers,' the cry goes up,
'Vengeance for Jacques Molay.' In cloud-pale rags, or in lace,
The rage-driven, rage-tormented, and rage-hungry troop,
Trooper belabouring trooper, biting at arm or at face,
Plunges towards nothing, arms and fingers spreading wide
For the embrace of nothing ...

But he is no longer a lofty Platonist, shadowing forth the 'daemonic rage'; he glimpses the abyss within himself:

> and I, my wits astray
> Because of all that senseless tumult, all but cried
> For vengeance on the murderers of Jacques Molay.

The next group, phantoms of the 'heart's fullness', provides an emotional antithesis:

> Their legs long, delicate and slender, aquamarine their eyes,
> Magical unicorns bear ladies on their backs.
> The ladies close their musing eyes. No prophecies,
> Remembered out of Babylonian almanacs,
> Have closed the ladies' eyes, their minds are but a pool
> Where even longing drowns under its own excess;
> Nothing but stillness can remain when hearts are full
> Of their own sweetness, bodies of their loveliness.

But this is not an ethical antithesis: these apparitions are not the invoked honeybees. Here one aspect of the self-sufficiency and self-delight which the speaker first projected into the fountain of 'Ancestral Houses' achieves final definition: not a fountain but a pool, not an abounding jet of life but an eternal stillness of self-contemplation. However beautiful, it is the deathly goal of Narcissus. For the living speaker these ladies and unicorns can image not a solution but one term of a predicament.

Indeed, they are strangely similar to their antitheses, the rage-driven troop: 'even longing drowns under its own excess'. Because the vision has moved from one blindness to another, from the ravenous imperception of Breughel's blindmen careering into the abyss to the closed eyes of Moreau's narcissistic women and unicorns,[15] it can now move easily, through an inversion of details further stressing that affinity, to a harshly empty synthesis:

> The cloud-pale unicorns, the eyes of aquamarine,
> The quivering half-closed eyelids, the rags of cloud or of lace,
> Or eyes that rage has brightened, arms it has made lean,
> Give place to the indifferent multitude, give place
> To brazen hawks.

Predatory rage and static self-satisfaction merge in a yet more terrible blindness:

> Nor self-delighting reverie,
> Nor hate of what's to come, nor pity for what's gone,
> Nothing but grip of claw, and the eye's complacency,

[15] For a more explicit image of the blindmen, see 'A Dialogue of Self and Soul', *Collected Poems*, p. 232, or 'On a Political Prisoner', *Collected Poems*, p. 181; for Yeats's possession of Moreau's 'Women and Unicorns', see *The Letters of W. B. Yeats*, ed. Allan Wade, [London, 1954], New York, 1955, p. 865.

The innumerable clanging wings that have put out the moon.

Such is the consummation the speaker envisions in modern history, such the consummation of his own ethical dialectic. Yet, though inescapably of his time, he is partly freed by the vision itself. He does not fully yield to the rage of the avenging troop, and he cannot now adopt the transcendent narcissism of aquamarine or closed eyes. The poem renders a precarious solution: not the imagined escape from the prison of self through freedom in love, but the open-eyed self-recognition of the half-trapped poet.

> I turn away and shut the door, and on the stair
> Wonder how many times I could have proved my worth
> In something that all others understand or share;
> But O! ambitious heart, had such a proof drawn forth
> A company of friends, a conscience set at ease,
> It had but made us pine the more.

The 'ambitious pains' which vexed him at the beginning of the poem cannot be escaped. The dialogical movement here as throughout the meditation—'But O! ambitious heart'—renders the speaker's alertness to the continual temptations to self-containment. It renders, therefore, his actual if momentary freedom from such self-containment. Because all images of fulfilment carry their own irony, he must accept the problematic human state, with its attendant guilt and dissatisfaction. And if life cannot in any facile way be self-delighting,

> The abstract joy,
> The half-read wisdom of daemonic images,
> Suffice the ageing man as once the growing boy.

The irony of 'suffice', which has led critics to comment upon Yeats's vacillation between action and contemplation or upon his 'unfortunate' dabbling in the occult, can be fully weighted only in the context of this rich meditation on what may and what may not suffice the heart. That irony implies no dismissal of the poetic task as 'mere dreams'. Nor is the speaker now Shelley's 'visionary prince' priding himself, through romantic irony, on 'mysterious wisdom won by toil'.[16] He is rather the fortunate victim of the 'daemonic images' we have just seen, which are for him the burden of self-knowledge. He no longer strives for the goal of action or that of fantasy—a substitute for action.

> The rhetorician would deceive his neighbours,
> The sentimentalist himself; while art
> Is but a vision of reality.[17]

The complex irony in that 'but', as in the 'suffice' of this poem, partly

---

[16] 'The Phases of the Moon', *Collected Poems*, p. 161.
[17] 'Ego Dominus Tuus', *Collected Poems*, p. 159.

answers any objection that 'Meditations in Time of Civil War' does not move to a clear ethical transcendence of the speaker's problem, as glimpsed in 'The Stare's Nest at My Window'. A willed vision of what the honeybees might bring would be factitious; the poet can realize only what he is. The rest may come of its own accord when, through being perceived, the psychic walls begin to crumble. Ribh would say, 'He holds him from desire'—and, indeed, the final section of this poem has rendered just such a 'symbolic revelation received after the suspension of desire' as 'What Magic Drum?' describes. 'Does not all art come', Yeats wrote, 'when a nature, that never ceases to judge itself, exhausts personal emotion in action or desire so completely that something impersonal . . . starts into its place, something which is as unforeseen, as completely organized, even as unique, as the images that pass before the mind between sleeping and waking?'[18] Such are the 'daemonic images' of this last section; such, in a larger sense, is the entire poem.

Despite Yeats's frequently quoted remarks about virtue as being dramatic, the wearing of a mask,[19] this poem renders his understanding of the fact that attention is the mother of virtue as it is of art. Though the speaker wears various masks of poetic or moral ambition, engages in the deceits of rhetorician and sentimentalist, he closely watches the self that does so. From that watching, that attention, spring both the ethical development of the speaker and the poem itself. For the poem, the 'vision of reality' is of that mask-wearing self, and it is therefore, like the poems of Villon, finally 'without fear or moral ambition' though decidedly ethical in its substance. In 1905, arguing against didactic art, art composed with the intent to persuade, Yeats had said:

> 'If we understand our own minds, and the things that are striving to utter themselves through our minds, we move others, not because we have understood or thought about those others, but because all life has the same root. Coventry Patmore has said, "The end of art is peace," and the following of art is little different from the following of religion in the intense preoccupation that it demands. Somebody has said, "God asks nothing of the highest soul except attention"; and so necessary is attention to mastery in any art, that there are moments when we think that nothing else is necessary, and nothing else so difficult.'[20]

Yeats clearly understood another of Patmore's statements: 'Attention to realities, rather than the fear of God, is "the beginning of wisdom" . . .' Given the bold prophetic note sounded by his art, we can see that he also might say with Patmore: 'Indeed, it is difficult to say how far an absolute moral courage in acknowledging intuitions may

[18] *Autobiographies*, p. 200.
[19] ibid., p. 285.
[20] *Plays and Controversies*, p. 161.

not be of the very nature of genius and whether it might not be described as a sort of interior sanctity which dares to see and confess to itself that it sees, though its vision should place it in a minority of one.'[21]

In 'Meditations in Time of Civil War', as in the apocalyptic romances of the nineties, a partial yielding to the daemonic voice enables the poet to perceive and judge those powers within him which, unconsciously obeyed, would lead and have led to historical catastrophe. But this poem of dramatic experience shows more clearly the complex interior dialogue through which suffering moves toward illumination, as the daemonic is incorporated into the precarious equilibrium of personality—and so transformed. The last sentence of the poem, ironically echoing Wordsworth's 'Ode on the Intimations of Immortality',[22] reinforces this conclusion. Wordsworth had said:

Shades of the prison-house begin to close
  Upon the growing Boy,
But He beholds the light, and whence it flows,
  He sees it in his joy . . .

And in compensation for the complete loss of that light, Wordsworth had found 'soothing thoughts that spring/Out of human suffering', a 'faith that looks through death', a 'philosophic mind'. But the Yeatsian speaker, aware of the Wordsworthian atrophy so rationalized, ironically affirms in his own life a lack of change, and so points to a more genuinely continuing growth:

  The abstract joy,
The half-read wisdom of daemonic images,
Suffice the ageing man as once the growing boy.

Though his continuing joy is 'abstract', an inevitable limitation arising from his turning inward to the source of daemonic images, the light shining through those images has led him to perceive the existence of his own prisonhouse, his chamber arched with stone, and to prevent it from closing upon him irrevocably. It has led him also to see that the 'philosophic mind', with *its* 'eye's complacency' is another form of the spiritual atrophy that tempts through every image that asks to be taken as a final truth, another phantom illustrating the multiform blindness which he precariously escapes. Perception must 'suffice', and full perception warns that our wisdom is momentary and but 'half-read'.

The symbolic rose, which here *breaks* in flower so diversely, cannot be forced. It must bloom in the midst of civil war: a unity of being that maintains the abounding jet of life must arise from the perception

---

[21] Coventry Patmore, *Principle in Art, and Religio Poetae*, one-vol. ed.; London, 1913, pp. 244, 290.

[22] As Richard Ellmann has suggested, *The Identity of Yeats*, London and New York, 1954, p. 223.

of disunity. No individual may complacently possess that fountain of life's self-delight. He may know it only through continuing openness, continuing vulnerability. Yeats had recognized as much, in a passage of 1917 which foreshadowed this poem:

'A poet, when he is growing old, will ask himself if he cannot keep his mask and his vision without new bitterness, new disappointment...

Surely, he may think, now that I have found vision and mask I need not suffer any longer. He will buy perhaps some small old house, where, like Ariosto, he can dig his garden, and think that in the return of birds and leaves, or moon and sun, and in the evening flight of the rooks he may discover rhythm and pattern like those in sleep and so never awake out of vision. Then he will remember Wordsworth withering into eighty years, honoured and empty-witted, and climb to some waste room and find, forgotten there by youth, some bitter crust.'[23]

And the speaker of 'Meditations in Time of Civil War' had guessed as much, near the beginning of the poem: 'Homer had not sung...' The *Iliad* offers no Goethean assurance of the eternal harmony of existence; indeed, Homer taught Goethe that in our life on earth we have, properly speaking, to enact Hell. The rose, finally, is the meditation itself, the spiritualization of that tragic soil, the vision of that state. For both the poet and the man, Yeats was discovering, the 'peace' of that vision is the paradoxically active means of transfiguring the wheel of destiny.

From *Swan and Shadow: Yeats's Dialogue with History*, Chapel Hill, the University of North Carolina Press, 1964, pp. 170–87.

[23] *Mythologies*, New York, 1959, p. 342.

F. A. C. WILSON

The Delphic Oracle upon Plotinus

This poem,[1] which a critic has called a 'gay and preposterous' joke,[2] and which is in fact one of the most profoundly serious of all Yeats's works, can best be seen for what it is by a reader acquainted with Porphyry's essay 'The Cave Of The Nymphs'.[3] Yeats felt that the influence of this essay on modern European art was considerable, maintaining (perhaps rightly) that Shelley's 'The Witch Of Atlas' and Botticelli's 'Nativity' were examples of works composed under its influence,[4] and he makes copious use of it in his own verse.

'The Cave Of The Nymphs' is ostensibly a commentary on the symbolism inherent in part of the *Odyssey*; though its value does not lie in the field of Homeric studies, but in the complete exegesis it affords of the Platonic system of symbolism. In Homer's poem, the wanderings of Odysseus end with his arrival at Phaeacia, a holy city exempt from war and the tyranny of the seasons; from there he sails home, crossing the sea in a Phaeacian boat, until he is brought to a cave on the coast of Ithaca. The cave is full of honeybees and honey is stored there; it is dedicated to the nymphs. This narrative[5] Porphyry interprets as a myth of the return of the soul, a parallel to the zodiacal symbolism I have referred to; and the starting point in his interpretation is the symbolic meaning attached to the sea-voyage. Platonism symbolizes the birth of the soul as its journey from the Isles of the Blessed in a celestial boat (the 'vehicle' in which the soul was thought to be contained); during life the soul is tossed about on the sea of emotion and passion; after death, living backwards through time, it recrosses the sea and returns to the island paradise from which it set out. All this symbolism can be read into the *Odyssey*, where the fruitless wanderings of Odysseus over the hostile sea are taken to symbolize the life of the unregenerate soul; his arrival at the holy city of Phaeacia, where it is perpetual spring, is read to mean the conversion of the soul to the intellectual life; and his return to Ithaca, to symbolize the soul's restoration to heaven, its native land, which can only be accomplished by virtue of the intellec-

---

[1] *Collected Poems* (henceforth *C.P.*), p. 306.
[2] W. Y. Tindall, in *The Symbolism Of W. B. Yeats*; reprinted from *Accent* in *The Permanence of Yeats*, p. 276.
[3] See Taylor, *Porphyry*, p. 171.
[4] See *Ideas of Good and Evil*, pp. 83–8; *A Vision*, A, p. 202.
[5] Homer, *Odyssey*, XIII; for Homer's cave, see XII, 92 et seq.

tual life.[6] With this in mind, Porphyry considers the significance of the cave at which Odysseus lands on what, for Platonism, is his return to the Isles of the Blessed; he takes it to be a symbol for the womb, or the matrix of generation, the threshold of the world. Through this gate the soul first descends into the material universe, and through it, it must reascend: its garment of flesh is woven on the looms the cave contains; the honey which is there is semen, or 'the pleasure arising from generation',[7] the honeybees and the nymphs who reside there are symbols for the two kinds of souls who are born into the world. All generated souls are nymphs, for a nymph is a water spirit, and thus a spirit in love with the sea of generation; but the honeybees are the souls of the just, for as Porphyry beautifully says 'this insect loves to return to the place from whence it came, and is eminently just and sober'.[8] Porphyry goes on to examine many other details of Homer's text, such as the amphorae and mixing-bowls which are in the cave; he interprets them all from the Platonic tradition, but I omit what is not relevant to Yeats.

Yeast knew and loved this once-famous essay, and he used many of its symbols in his own verse. 'Honey of generation' occurs in 'Among School Children' and is referred to Porphyry by a note,[9] and where this is so we are justified in interpreting 'The Stare's Nest At My Window' from the same source:

We have fed the heart on fantasies,
The heart's grown brutal from the fare;
More substance in our enmities
Than in our love: O honey-bees,
Come build in the empty house of the stare.[10]

The honey-bees, I take it, are the souls of the just, and Yeats is praying for the return of justice to an Ireland ravaged by civil war. His poetry is equally full of symbolism of the sea-voyage to and from perfection: 'things out of perfection sail',[11] 'Swift has sailed into his rest',[12] and the poet himself has 'crossed the seas' and come to 'the holy city of Byzantium',[13] a city which is surely reminiscent of Phaeacia. In the present poem, the symbolism of the sea-voyage is the link with 'The Cave Of The Nymphs', but in Yeats's sequel, 'News For The Delphic Oracle', the whole of Porphyry's essay is relevant, and this is why I have reconstructed it at length here.

'The Delphic Oracle Upon Plotinus' is an original poem based upon the verse-oracle delivered to Amelius after the death of Plotinus,

[6] See Taylor, *Porphyry*, pp. 241 ff.
[7] ibid., p. 183.
[8] ibid., p. 185; quoted in *Ideas of Good and Evil*, p. 85.
[9] *C.P.*, p. 535 (note).
[10] *C.P.*, p. 230.
[11] 'Old Tom Again', *C.P.*, p. 306.
[12] 'Swift's Epitaph', *C.P.*, p. 277.
[13] 'Sailing To Byzantium', *C.P.*, p. 217.

which as it happens is preserved, with a commentary, in Porphyry's *Life*.[14] The Greek original of this poem has always been much loved by Platonists, and Yeats knew the translations by Taylor and MacKenna, as he did the additional commentary by Henry More.[15] The oracle is addressed to Plotinus himself, and describes his journey over the sea of life to the Isles of the Blessed; after death Plotinus does not have to recross the sea by expiating his memories, for his life has had the purity of a saint's. Living as he did 'in the sleepless vision within and without',[16] he had nothing to expiate. On his death, then, he is free to 'enter at once the heavenly consort': but he has had to struggle against the sea during life, when he was sustained by visionary experience:

> 'Oft-times as you strove to rise above the bitter waves of this blood-drenched life, above the sickening whirl, toiling in the midmost of the rushing flood and the unimaginable turmoil, oft-times, from the Ever Blessed, there was shown to you the term still close at hand. . . .
>
> But now that you have cast the screen aside, quitted the tomb that held your lofty soul, you enter at once the heavenly consort:
>
> Where fragrant breezes play, where all is unison and winning tenderness and guileless joy, and the place is lavish of the nectar-streams the unfailing Gods bestow, with the blandishments of the loves, and delicious airs, and tranquil sky.
>
> Where Minos and Rhadamanthus dwell, great brethren of the golden race of mighty Zeus; where dwells the just Aeacus, and Plato, concentrated power, and stately Pythagoras and all else that form the choir of immortal love, there where the heart is ever lifted in joyous festival.'[17]

While Plotinus lived, he was in visionary contact with reality, 'the term still close at hand', and after death he was admitted at once to the company of philosophers, musicians and lovers who make up, with the immortals, and the three judges of the dead, the number of 'the golden race'. His death was instant transfiguration: 'then the term ever near was vouchsafed to Plotinus', as Porphyry beautifully says.[18]

It may not be apparent why the company of heaven should consist so exclusively of philosophers, musicians and lovers; and it is worth clarifying this point, for to do so will explain why Yeats used his poem as he did, to serve as the end-paper to *Words For Music Perhaps*. I will quote Henry More's commentary, which was favourite

---

[14] In MacKenna, *Plotinus*, I, p. 22.
[15] *A Collection Of Several Philosophical Writings Of Henry More* (1662), p. 181.
[16] MacKenna, op. cit., I, p. 24.
[17] ibid., p. 23.
[18] ibid. But I use Taylor's wording of the translation.

reading for Yeats. In Heaven, More says, the soul's occupation consists:

> 'not only in rational discourses, which is so agreeable to the Philosophical Ingeny, but innocent Pastimes, in which the Musical and Amorous propension may be also recreated. For these Three dispositions are the flower of all the rest, as Plotinus has somewhere noted.'[19]

In fact Plotinus wrote a long essay to show that the metaphysician, musician and lover are the three kinds of men most capable of visionary experience, and thus of cultivating the intellectual life and obtaining release from the cycle of material existence, 'the metaphysician taking to the path by instinct, the musician and the nature peculiarly susceptible to love needing outside guidance'.[20] Yeats knew the text in Plotinus, of course, as well as he did More's interpretation of the oracle, and it made his poem peculiarly apposite to the theme of *Words For Music Perhaps*. In his song-cycle, Yeats's beggar-woman and journeyman are tragically conscious that their love is something outside time, and must wait until they themselves are outside time for its consummation:

> What can be shown?
> What true love be?
> All could be known or shown
> If time were but gone.
> *'That's certainly the case,' said he.*[21]

Plotinus, as Houghton points out,[22] had given Yeats precedent for believing that the soul continued its individual existence in heaven; and the authorities I have quoted give him Platonic authority that it would consummate its love there. Yeats ends all his song-cycles with a classical text in paraphrase that will bear out his main arguments in the cycle as a whole, and he does so here: the heaven so much desired by Plotinus is also that desired by Jack the Journeyman and Crazy Jane, where they will consummate their spiritual union:

> There stately Pythagoras
> And all the choir of love.

I see nothing inept in this treatment, which is for me a mark of the nobility of Yeats's thought: 'everything that lives is holy', and the soul of his ragged beggar-woman is as much a 'beautiful lofty thing' as that of Plotinus. Through love, she has the same vision of her source.

[19] More, op. cit., p. 181.
[20] MacKenna, I, p. 51.
[21] 'Crazy Jane On The Day Of Judgment', *C.P.*, p. 291.
[22] W. E. Houghton: 'Yeats And Crazy Jane'; reprinted from *Modern Philology* in *The Permanence Of Yeats*, p. 381.

In Yeats's poem, the soul of man, under the figure of Plotinus, is seen proceeding to its consummation, the consummation which has been glimpsed in visionary experience by Jack and Crazy Jane. Yeats begins with an image of characteristic levity, but it is levity of the kind Goethe characterizes as *holder Leichtsinn*, tragic levity not meant to detract from the essential seriousness of the whole:

> Behold that great Plotinus swim,
> Buffeted by such seas;

This is an unexpected development of an earlier prose passage, where Yeats, talking of the Platonic sea, had characterized man as 'a swimmer, or rather the waves themselves';[23] and it startles, even shocks; but it gives Yeats the dynamic impact his poem needs (and which MacKenna's translation of the original Greek perhaps lacks). Yeats pares down his Greek text for the sake of concision, and proceeds at once to the heart of his theme, balancing his levity against his tragic purpose. The faint insolence of the following 'bland', and the sharp impact of the verse's close, are merged, now, into the growing dignity of the whole:

> Bland Rhadamanthus beckons him,
> But the Golden Race looks dim,
> Salt blood blocks his eyes.

We have to remember that Plotinus is travelling across the sea of life, and has no knowledge of his destination save what he can glimpse from visionary experience; he has, for a moment, a fragmentary perception of his goal, but it vanishes; the contaminating salt of material concerns, flung up into his eyes from the sea, half blinds him to what he has perceived. This is a development of part of the oracle I have not quoted, which describes how, during life, Plotinus' eyes sometimes grew 'dim' to visions, and his mind was 'rapt down unsanctioned paths'.[24] Rhadamanthus is one of the three judges of the dead, and there may be significance in the fact that he, and not Aeacus or Minos, is Plotinus' guide. We are told in Plato's *Gorgias*[25] that Rhadamanthus judges the souls who come from Asia, and Plotinus can be thought of, if we choose, as in a sense Asiatic: he is a product of the Christian dispensation, which in Yeats's system is an Asiatic influx, and determines the essential nature of all the souls born into it.[26] I do not think it is necessary to take this reading; but I would not care to say outright that Yeats did not intend it.

The remainder of the poem needs no further commentary; its function as argument is to people Yeats's heaven. Plato is given as the

---

[23] *Wheels and Butterflies*, p. 73.
[24] MacKenna, I, p. 23.
[25] Plato, *Gorgias*, 524.
[26] For this point see Ellmann, *The Identity Of Yeats*, p. 281; and *A Vision*, B, p. 203.

type of the philosopher; Pythagoras, surrounded by his 'immortal choir', appears in the character of master-musician; and Yeats completes More's argument by making it clear that the singers are 'the choir of love':

> Scattered on the level grass
> Or winding through the grove
> Plato there and Minos pass,
> There stately Pythagoras
> And all the choir of love.

All that I need do is to notice the simplicity and dignity of the presentation, the quiet opening lines rising to a pitch of some excitement with the exclamatory 'there' of the fourth line, where Yeats varies his rhythm, only to restore it in the calm composure of his conclusion, with its air of confident hope. I find 'The Delphic Oracle Upon Plotinus' peculiarly moving, and I think it is technically one of the most perfect of Yeats's lyrics.

From *W. B. Yeats and Tradition*, London: Gollancz, 1958, pp. 211–16.

DENIS DONOGHUE

Words for Music Perhaps

> Whatever stands in field or flood,
> Bird, beast, fish or man,
> Mare or stallion, cock or hen,
> Stands in God's unchanging eye
> In all the vigour of its blood;
> In that faith I live or die.
>
> from 'Tom the Lunatic' (1931)

Reading Yeats, we would posit a poet who suffered from a psychosis characteristic of our time and familiar to other times: namely, an intense and painful preoccupation with the seemingly irreconcilable claims of Soul and Body. Intense and painful, because being a poet he was driven, as by an entelechial motive typical of the artist, toward images of wholeness, unity, and perfection. There seemed no possibility, however, of realizing or enacting 'Unity of Being': the poetic metaphor was frustrate at every point. In 'King and No King' he had written:

> And I that have not your faith, how shall I know
> That in the blinding light beyond the grave,
> We'll find so good a thing as that we have lost?
> The hourly kindness, the day's common speech,
> The habitual content of each with each
> When neither soul nor body has been crossed.

Thus Yeats as *sufferer*. As *agent* he sought to heal himself: first, by the sheer act of lamenting the lost harmony, working within the optative mood, describing great-rooted chestnut-trees that suffered from none of man's antinomies. Second, and more characteristic: with a dramatist's instinct he broke down the psychosis into its two great conflicting parts, thereafter interpreting experience, as his mood or 'condition' prodded, now in terms of Soul (or Spirit or Essence), now in terms of Body (or Nature or Circumstance). The psychosis was a complex and unmanageable simultaneity: Yeats replaced it, imperatively, by a more tolerable scheme of successiveness. He resolved a contradictory 'yes-no' by setting up a plot that developed from 'yes' to 'no' and *vice versa*.[1]

[1] *Cf.* Kenneth Burke: 'Mysticism as a Solution to the Poet's Dilemma', Stanley Romaine Hopper (ed.), *Spiritual Problems in Contemporary Literature*, Harper, 1952. This seems an appropriate moment to acknowledge a debt to Mr Burke which extends through and beyond the present essay.

In *The Wanderings of Oisin, Crossways, The Rose* and *The Wind Among the Reeds*, Yeats located the Spirit in a realm of picturesque sorrow with 'numberless islands', 'many a Danaan shore', and a 'woven world-forgotten isle'. In those books whatever mode of existence is for the time being identified with the Spirit is protected, in tenderness, from the onslaught of Body or Nature. Those early poems are a long and intermittently beautiful yes-saying to the Spirit; but the Spirit is abused, maimed, because torn from the Body. In later years and with different materials Yeats frequently said 'yes' to the Spirit; under the guise of Mind, for instance, as in 'All Souls' Night':

Such thought—such thought have I that hold it tight
Till meditation master all its parts,
Nothing can stay my glance
Until that glance run in the world's despite
To where the damned have howled away their hearts,
And where the blessed dance:
Such thought, that in it bound
I need no other thing,
Wound in mind's wandering
As mummies in the mummy-cloth are wound.

In this poem Yeats praises those adepts who, like Florence Emery, meditate upon unknown thought and repudiate the Body:

What matter who it be,
So that his elements have grown so fine
The fume of muscatel
Can give his sharpened palate ecstasy
No living man can drink from the whole wine.

Ours, in fact, are 'gross palates'.

Thus one situation, one stage in the entire plot. Its counterpart is the Crazy Jane series of poems in *Words for Music Perhaps*.

The year is 1929: Yeats is recovering from an attack of Maltese fever. Behind him, or so he fancies, are the world of politics, the old Irish Senate, the 'no petty people' speech, and 'a sixty-year-old smiling public man'. He writes to Olivia Shakespeare from Rapallo: 'No more opinions, no more politics, no more practical tasks'. Joyful riddance: it is a prosperous moment. Sixty-four years old, Yeats feels new strength and sexual energy returning to his body. He is impelled to have recourse to that 'nature' (in bodily, even in fecal terms) from which he had withdrawn, estranged, to a more 'gracious' world of pure Mind. Now he withdraws again, provisionally, not only from pure Mind but from a 'practical' scene of disillusion and defeat. Ridding himself of a 'practical' world he reduces his *scene* accordingly: he identifies his will, provisionally, with the urges of the body giving to it (for protection and definition) the name Crazy Jane.

It is a simplification and therefore an evasion. Indeed each of Yeats's books of poems is a provisional simplification, a trial account of his universe devoted not to the entire complex truth but to a particular bias or impetus which is, for the time being, dominant. Some of Yeats's books are 'phoenix' books: others are 'turtle' books: what one longs for is the mutual flame:

> Hearts remote, yet not asunder;
> Distance, and no space was seen.

In the Crazy Jane poems, for instance, Yeats for the time being places as much trust in the biologic (a turtle, surely) as Racine had placed in the greatly passionate, or Wordsworth in the greatly sensitive. Otherwise stated, the biological imperative, as a principle of structure, is the 'myth' of the Crazy Jane poems, corresponding to the anthropological myth of *The Waste Land*. This position, downward-tending in its images, is close to that of Lawrence in *Lady Chatterley's Lover*.

Words for Music Perhaps: the words are for music, not because they are to be sung, but because their burden, like that of the ballad, belongs to the *folk*. Indeed it is perhaps not too inaccurate to say that the book enacts that quantity of folk-experience which has 'the body's potencies' (Lawrence's phrase) as its prime motive.

We must try to get the connotations right. It is called 'that foul body' in 'Those Dancing Days Are Gone', but we must be careful to watch the context. Careful, above all, not to argue from such references that (as a critic has recently maintained) Yeats even in the Crazy Jane poems 'identifies the physical, corporeal aspects of love with that which is *foul*'; or that in his later poems, going one better, he 'regards the sexual act as mostly beastly'. There is a curious tonality in these poems to which the reader should respond:

> Come, let me sing into your ear;
> Those dancing days are gone,
> All that silk and satin gear;
> Crouch upon a stone,
> Wrapping that foul body up
> In as foul a rag:
> *I carry the sun in a golden cup,*
> *The moon in a silver bag.*

The reference is specific. The human body as such is not foul: what is foul is, in this context, its decay—the loss of that power, mainly sexual ('the vigour of its blood'), which Yeats frequently symbolized in terms of the dance. Six days before writing this poem Yeats had rendered that power in 'Crazy Jane Grown Old Looks at the Dancers':

F

God be with the times when I
Cared not a thraneen for what chanced
So that I had the limbs to try
Such a dance as there was danced—
Love is like the lion's tooth.

Again in 'Mad as the Mist and Snow' the winds are foul because
they testify to decay. In 'All Souls' Night' the years are foul because
they enforce decay on Florence Emery's beauty:

And knowing that the future would be vexed
With 'minished beauty, multiplied commonplace,
Preferred to teach a school
Away from neighbour or friend,
Among dark skins, and there
Permit foul years to wear
Hidden from eyesight to the unnoticed end.

Indeed Yeats uses the word most characteristically when he has in
mind sheer *mutability*: the connotations of the word are pathetic, not
dyslogistic or censorial. The trickiest case is, of course, 'Crazy Jane
Talks with the Bishop', but even here the rhetoric of the poem seeks
to redeem the word:

I met the Bishop on the road
And much said he and I.
   'Those breasts are flat and fallen now,
   Those veins must soon be dry;
   Live in a heavenly mansion,
   Not in some foul sty.'

The choice is offered as if its terms were unanswerable: the Bishop,
as rhetorician, has no time for the Gidean problematic. Here, of course,
'foul' is censorial, and we may expect the Bishop to be whipped for
his cliché. Crazy Jane accepts the word, and its challenge, but redeems
its meaning:

'Fair and foul are near of kin,
And fair needs foul,' I cried.
'My friends are gone, but that's a truth
Nor grave nor bed denied,
Learned in bodily lowliness
And in the heart's pride.'

There is also, she claims, the God of Love, who has his own rights,
his own idea of decorum, and his own mansion. Furthermore, the
terms which He proffers have a sanction prior to that of the Bishop's

God; prior, because they are 'justified' by the axioms of the body
and by 'the heart's pride':

> A woman can be proud and stiff
> When on love intent;
> But Love has pitched his mansion in
> The place of excrement;
> For nothing can be sole or whole
> That has not been rent.

A devotee of Blake, she has the last word.

She has the first word in 'Crazy Jane on the Day of Judgment',
and here her interpretation of love has a wider circumference than
is characteristic of her. Indeed the Crazy Jane of this poem encompas-
ses the three great dramatic roles through which, as Richard Ellmann
has observed, Yeats voiced his conceptions. First, she is the Seer:

> 'Love is all
> Unsatisfied
> That cannot take the whole
> Body and soul';

Then the Victim:

> 'Naked I lay,
> The grass my bed;
> Naked and hidden away,
> That black day';

Finally, the Assessor:

> 'What can be shown?
> What true love be?
> All could be known or shown
> If Time were but gone.'

The poem is intensely moving because it enacts the impulse to test
the possibilities of growth and extension in a conception of love
based on the bodily imperative. Crazy Jane's speculations do not get
very far, and anything like an Incarnational view of the body is as
far beyond her range as beyond Yeats's at any point: but in this
poem there is an urge to face ultimate questions which is frequently
evaded in *Words for Music Perhaps*. This book is devoted, as by
programme, to a partial view of things: Crazy Jane has a deeper
conception of love than Jack the Journeyman, but she is less urgently
engaged in refining this conception than in knocking down Aunt
Sallies like the Bishop. In the later *Supernatural Songs* Ribh plays
a similar role: not so much enacting the *whole* as insisting on the

part which, he asserts, the Christian idea discards: 'the phallic consciousness', again Lawrence's phrase:

> Natural and supernatural with the self-same ring are wed.
> As man, as beast, as an ephemeral fly begets, Godhead begets
>   Godhead,
> For things below are copies, the Great Smaragdine Tablet said.

Crazy Jane and Ribh are propagandists: they speak half-truths, by
vocation. Their position may be more 'right' than that of the Bishop,
but they exhibit—just as he does—a degree of incompleteness, or
*dis*unity, which puts the poetic metaphor beyond their grasp. The
speaker in 'All Souls' Night' is a Paleface; Crazy Jane and Ribh are
Redskins (to use Philip Rahv's terms), 'countering the sensibility' of
'The Tower' with their own 'experience'. But the experience itself is
raw, and therefore liable to face in its own turn an ironical if not
destructive scrutiny. 'Rawness' of experience and 'thinness' of experience are both in danger of mockery. The Cossack is the Jew's
critic: the Jew returns the stare.

Yeats wanted his 'Poems for Music' to be 'all emotion and all
impersonal'. On March 2, 1929 (the day on which he composed
'Crazy Jane and the Bishop' and 'Crazy Jane Grown Old Looks at the
Dancers'), he referred to the poems: 'They are the opposite of my
recent work and all praise of joyous life, though in the best of them
it is a dry bone on the shore that sings the praise.' Joyous life in this
book is life in which the primary commitment is to the body. Everything else may change or be dissolved, but not that.

Thus far the book as 'self-expression'. But we would insinuate
another perspective, a rhetorical one, involving the persuasive relation
between the poet and his audience.

Reading Yeats we would posit a poet who, 'believing in' none of
the public, institutional faiths, yet needing their public status and
the impact of their authority, used each, for the time being, according
as he felt that one of its characteristic patterns of insight was specially
pertinent to the situation to be rendered in the poem. He may indeed
have been drawn to see this 'point' by recognizing a formal or aesthetic
congruity between the 'pattern' in the institutional context and the
putative pattern in front of him as a poet. Thus the 'use' of the Way
of the Cross in 'The Travail of Passion' to guarantee feeling akin to
its own:

> When the flaming lute-thronged angelic door is wide;
> When an immortal passion breathes in mortal clay;
> Our hearts endure the scourge, the plaited thorns, the way
> Crowded with bitter faces, the wounds in palm and side,
> The vinegar-heavy sponge, the flowers by Kedron stream;
> We will bend down and loosen our hair over you,
> That it may drop faint perfume, and be heavy with dew,
> Lilies of death-pale hope, roses of passionate dream.

Correspondingly, Yeats's recourse to the biologic in the 'Crazy Jane' poems is an invocation to a pattern of experience which has the force of public status, complete with dogmas, rites, mysteries and imperatives—and this by universal assent. The great advantage of the biological imperative as a source of verbal communication is that it is *prior* to all conflicts of thought or belief: it undercuts the more contentious levels of experience.

Yeats's instinct for communication on such terms was keen, though often diverted locally by pressure from other sources. No one knew better than he that meditations upon unknown thought make human intercourse grow less and less. In 1906 he spoke of the two ways before literature, 'the way of the bird until common eyes have lost us or to the market carts'. The choice, as thus presented, is too *simpliste* to be acceptable, and it is possible to argue that Yeats was too readily persuaded toward the market carts by the expressive resources of common idiom. But it is clear that certain associations were formed in his mind: linguistic vigour, John Millington Synge, common speech, folk-wisdom, and a mode of life founded on the body and the soil. These realities had a way of calling to each other in his mind. In the 1930 Diary, for instance—in the middle of the Crazy Jane period—he wrote:

> 'The use of dialect for the expression of the most subtle emotion—Synge's translation of Petrarch—verse where the syntax is that of common life, are but the complement of a philosophy spoken in the common idiom escaped from isolating method, gone back somehow from professor and pupil to Blind Tiresias.'

Here Yeats shares the motive behind Synge's exaltation of Villon, Herrick and Burns in the Preface to *Poems and Translations*. The same motive determines to a large extent the syntax and diction which we find in the later poems and plays.

We have posited a strategic simplification and called it evasion. And we would guess further that a great mind which has recourse to such a strategy can do so only with severe misgivings, knowing that it must omit so much, condone so much distortion. *The Tower* is splendid poetry mainly because in building its Holy City it cannot bring itself to leave the recalcitrant (the 'downward' tending) out of account. The later books cut the knots more ruthlessly. That is why one has the disconcerting feeling, reading the later books, that Yeats is adopting certain roles because he rather fancies himself in the parts. A new and distressing kind of picturesque, it leads to a certain hardening of the arteries in such a poem as 'News for the Delphic Oracle'. The first stanza goes:

> There all the golden codgers lay,
> There the silver dew,
> And the great water sighed for love,

And the wind sighed too.
Man-picker Niamh leant and sighed
By Oisin on the grass;
There sighed amid his choir of love
Tall Pythagoras.
Plotinus came and looked about,
The salt-flakes on his breast,
And having stretched and yawned awhile
Lay sighing like the rest.

Porphyry's Elysian Fields are very like Yeats's Island of Forgetfulness, and Yeats (sly old virtuoso) can now jeer at both. With the same virtuosity he can laugh at the equestrian Innocents: he could never take innocence seriously, anyway:

Straddling each a dolphin's back
And steadied by a fin,
Those Innocents re-live their death,
Their wounds open again.
The ecstatic waters laugh because
Their cries are sweet and strange,
Through their ancestral patterns dance,
And the brute dolphins plunge
Until, in some cliff-sheltered bay
Where wades the choir of love
Proffering its sacred laurel crowns,
They pitch their burdens off.

The last word is Yeats's: he offers it, surely, as critique:

Slim adolescence that a nymph has stripped,
Peleus on Thetis stares.
Her limbs are delicate as an eyelid,
Love has blinded him with tears;
But Thetis' belly listens.
Down the mountain walls
From where Pan's cavern is
Intolerable music falls.
Foul goat-head, brutal arm appear,
Belly, shoulder, bum,
Flash fishlike; nymphs and satyrs
Copulate in the foam.

Touché. Yes, but isn't it, itself, in a weak position, despite the biological imperative? The poem has ended, but one could envisage a fourth stanza (written by Dante) in which the Yeatsian heaven of the third would be shown for the vulnerable thing it is. The critique, the corrective, is valid enough as far as it goes, but not sufficiently valid to justify the *tone*, the shrill, exhibitionist mockery.

We would argue that the shrillness of Yeats's later work testifies to those misgivings which we posited at an earlier stage in our essay. In *Words for Music Perhaps* Yeats's recourse to simplification places him in a false position which issues in the poems as a certain stridency, a tendency to shout.

Yeats soon got tired of Crazy Jane, thus perhaps acknowledging the limited range of her insights. He used her once again, innocuously, cursing puny times and a world bereft of Cuchulains.

Words for Music Perhaps is valuable because it enables us to re-enact a 'movement of the psyche' downward into the limited, finite *thing*. The movement is touching in itself, in its compulsions and its embarrassments: only the most thick-skinned reader could fail to be moved and disturbed by this (partial) image of the human condition. The pathos of the book is that when Yeats had reached down deeply into the finite Body there was little he could do with it: he saw no means of penetrating the finite without transcending it; and thereby destroying it, as Roderick destroyed Madeline, in a rage for Essence.

From ' "The Vigour of Its Blood": Yeats's *Words for Music Perhaps*', *Kenyon Review,* Vol. XXI, 1959, pp. 376–87.

VIVIENNE KOCH

The Gyres

I should like to preface what I consider a relevant, although certainly not an exclusive, reading of this difficult poem by a few general remarks which have a bearing on it. Back in the nineties, Yeats may have been struck by the word 'gyre' in a poem of Francis Thompson's which evidently made a deep impression on him for he quotes it thirty years later in *A Vision*. The subject-matter of the quoted passage is, moreover, remarkably close to the main idea of Yeats's 'system' as set down in *A Vision*:

> Not only of cyclic Man
> Thou here discern'st the plan,
> Not only of cyclic Man, but of the cyclic Me
> Not only of Immortalities great years
>   The reflex just appears
> But thine own bosom's year, still circling round
> In ample and in ampler gyre
> Towards the far completion, wherewith crowned
> Love unconsumed shall chant on his own funeral pyre.

Perhaps the earliest use of 'gyre' in Yeats's own poetry was in the superb opening of 'The Second Coming', written in 1919:

> Turning and turning in the widening gyre
> The falcon cannot hear the falconer;

Related poems of the same period turn up a frequent use of the word,[1] and it continues to appear in some of the best poems of the following decade,[2] until by 1935, the probable date of the composition of 'The Gyres', the gyres themselves become the subject matter of the poem.

We can trace, then, how Thompson's conjunction of the gyre symbol with his notion of 'cyclic Man' had, by the time of the writing of *A Vision* in the early twenties, taken on a deepened meaning for Yeats. It was in 1929 that he wrote from Shillingford to his friend, Mrs Shakespeare, that he was searching out signs of the whirling gyres of the historical cones in occult books such as Mrs Strong's *Apotheosis and After-Life,* and that by studying them he hoped to see deeper into what was to come. 'My own philosophy', he added, 'does not much brighten the prospects so far as any future we shall

---

[1] See 'Demon and Beast' and 'Shepherd and Goatherd'.
[2] See 'All Souls' Night' and 'Byzantium'.

live.' By the time of the composition of 'The Gyres' fourteen years later, his pessimism was even more profound. And, significantly, it is at about this time that in his letters to Dorothy Wellesley Yeats talks of the spirits of the dead in folklore who are represented as being enveloped in a whirlwind. This whirling metaphor is expanded in 'The Gyres' to embrace the cyclic movement of history which includes not only the spirits of the dead, but dead cultures and civilizations as well.

And, if we must further unravel the complex web of associations which the symbol of the gyre carried for Yeats, there are many useful passages in *A Vision*, which point to the common element present in *all* the uses of the word which I have indicated. Thus, for example, in the amusing faked introduction to that alleged mystical book of the sixteenth century, Yeats wrote:

'The anguish of birth and death cry out in the same instant. Life is no series of emanations from divine reason such as the Cabalists imagine, but an irrational bitterness, no orderly descent from level to level, no waterfall but a whirlpool, a gyre.'

Later, Yeats attempts to trace various mentions of gyres in antiquity, through Aquinas and up to Swedenborg. All these 'historical' gyres appear to share two elements in common: circular movement and a combination of two opposite movements. Without detaining ourselves to expound the questionable structure of Yeats's 'system', it is nevertheless important to understand that he sees his cones and gyres as the *principles* of energy which move the Four Faculties, and which generate the patterns of their movements. I do not think that anyone has pointed out that this creative antagonism of opposites which Yeats makes the axis of his cosmology is really an extension of his early and presumably abandoned theory of the Mask, a theory originally centred in the value of conflict to the creative imagination, but now universalized into a dynamic principle which accounts for both human and superhuman growth. That the early vision of this belief was unconsciously working towards its later enlargement is indicated by a revealing passage in 'The Trembling of the Veil', the section of Yeats's *Autobiographies* which deals with the years between 1887 and 1891:

'My mind began drifting vaguely towards the doctrine of "the mask" which convinced me that ever-passionate man ... is, as it were, linked with another age historical or imaginary, where he alone finds images that rouse his energy.'

Now, while these symbolic analogues of Yeats are often arbitrary, unclear, and even absurd, they must be regarded as the efforts of a rich but unsophisticated mind to work out an ethos and a psychology that would order its multiple and perplexing experience. Oddly enough, Yeats was sufficiently given over to a long habit of introspection about his own thought-processes to be aware of this. He had written to his father just before his marriage in 1917 that he was working out a religious system which was helping his verse by giving him a 'framework of patterns'. And the profound intellectual therapy of this effort—'getting the disorder of one's mind in order'—Yeats put as co-evalent with 'the real impulse to create'.

Before I attempt to weight the 'philosophic' gravity of 'The Gyres' as an expression of the will-to-order which Yeats equated with the poetic function, I should like to make a technical study of its construction. And I do not for a moment suggest that such an inspection is incidental to the other end. On the contrary, if there is a 'philosophic' import to be got from the poem, this is the only way I know to get at it. For we can then feel confident that the 'philosophy' has been precipitated by the *facts* of the poem, rather than by our secondary sources of knowledge concerning Yeats's beliefs.

The opening injunction of 'The Gyres' is unambiguous:

> The gyres! the gyres! Old Rocky Face, look forth;
> Things thought too long can be no longer thought.

The gyres, a cosmic phenomenon, are pointed to as event, much as one would call attention to a comet trailing the sky. It is Old Rocky Face who is enjoined to watch. Old Rocky Face is the poet, wearing a very transparent mask. It is he, Yeats, who is old, rocky; it is he, Yeats (stanza two), who is the 'lover of horses and women' and not Shelley's Jew. And the voice that is calling Rocky Face is that 'antithetical self', the poet in his other, prophetic guise. This conclusion is supported by the many poems of the last phase written in the form of an interior dialogue. 'The Man and the Echo', which we shall study as a companion piece to this poem, employs an objective dialogue structure; the voice of 'The Gyres' is a single one which, by a narrative rhetoric, talks for the suppressed aspect of the self here called 'Old Rocky Face'. A dialogue of the self and the anti-self, 'Ego Dominus Tuus', written in 1915, shows how early this strategy of dramatizing the conflicts of personality by splitting off the warring elements into fictive personae suggested itself to Yeats. Excitingly, it is in this very poem, written two decades before 'The Gyres', that we find an image which is the prototype of Rocky Face: the reference is to Dante:

> I think he fashioned from his opposite
> An image that might have been a stony face.

By the time Yeats comes to write 'The Gyres' and 'The Man and the Echo', it is himself he sees as the stony face. In a draft of the latter poem which he enclosed in a note to Dorothy Wellesley, the Man addresses the Echo as 'O rocky void'. In the printed version it becomes—and the capitals are significant—'O Rocky Voice'. This is the poet addressing his antiself, Echo. 'Rocky Face' in 'The Gyres' is the identical element in his personality, but deprived of his speaking voice. In this connection it is interesting to note that both poems are alike indebted to a cavern or tomb atmosphere. And, if we must bring Shelley in, it might better be in the distinction Yeats had made in 1900 between his symbols of tower and cave: 'The contrast between it (the tower) and the cave', he had written, '... suggests a contrast between the mind looking outward upon men and things and the mind looking inward upon itself....' Yeats adds that these associations may or may not have been in Shelley's mind. Certainly they existed in his own.

The pervasiveness of the tower symbol in the poetry of the twenties —significantly, the first decade of his marriage—when Yeats appeared to be at last achieving a relatively outward adjustment, is to be contrasted with the epithets of the thirties, the Rocky Voices, and the Rocky Faces. The conclusion is inevitable and almost every one of the *Last Poems* tends to urge it: the closing years of his life threw Yeats back upon his introspective habit with an additional intensity possibly effected by the temporary revitalization of sexuality. Thus, it was with a more troubled consciousness of the complexity of this process of 'the mind looking inward upon itself' that these poems were written. They were, moreover, a description of the *action* of this process itself.

The fiction of 'The Gyres', then, is the fiction of the split person. And the ecstatic voice which urges Old Rocky Face to 'look forth' is the voice of Yeats's other self. I have mentioned Dr Jeffares's list of 'key-words', but of these I can accept only 'gyres' as a true one. For if the whole notion of 'key-words' is not to become another mechanical short-cut in the reading of poetry, it must be reserved for those words about which cluster the emotional centres of the poem. The mere fact of the *repetition* of a word does not in itself, as Dr Jeffares and some others appear to suppose, constitute a key-word. On the foregoing definition, I should add to 'gyres', as genuine key-words, 'blood', 'stain' and 'cavern'. But if my own series is to stand as a more than arbitrary choice, it must be elucidated.

'Blood' is central to stanza one and, at a reduced intensity, to stanza two. The total atmosphere of the first stanza is one of destruction, chaos and terror. Against this is put the great cyclic energy of the gyres, which, as they whirl away the memory of the ancient lineaments, and refine away the vitality of an unreplenished art and morality, foreshadow, if by no other means than the exclamation points which announce them, some kind of positive deliverance.

'Stain', while a true key-word, does not work solely by its own power but in conjunction with 'blood'. 'The irrational streams of blood ... Staining earth' point to a cosmic cataclysm. Stanza two narrows this holocaust to a statement of the individual's dishonour: 'And blood and mire the sensitive body stain', thus permitting the poet to speak in his own voice in the lines:

For painted forms or boxes of make-up
In ancient tombs I sighed, but not again;

Phonetically, both 'blood' and 'stain' are strong words. In addition, they are so positioned that they inherit the metrical emphasis of the line.

'Cavern' is a less obvious key-word. In a later poem, 'Those Images', one of the most balanced, healthy, and ideologically clear of the *Last Poems*, the Mind is told to leave its 'caverns', for

There's better exercise
In the sunlight and wind.[3]

In 'The Gyres', 'cavern' is used only once and its position is not as distinctive metrically as those of the key-words we have just looked at. But it reinforces, and indeed, is a *part* of the symbol of 'Old Rocky Face', an epithet for those elements in the self which Yeats associates with the congealed areas of personality, 'Things thought too long can be no longer thought'. In addition, the 'cavern' represents the layer of personality most inaccessible to consciousness, but which yet increases itself by this neglect, pushing its way into the conscious mind and there dictating its demands seemingly 'against' reason.

But the cavern metaphor serves Yeats as yet another level of argument in *A Vision* where it is a kind of metaphysical archetype. In one of the strangest passages in that dubious concoction, Yeats wrote:

'At or near the central point of a lunar month of classical civiliza- tion . . . came the Christian primary dispensation, the child born in the Cavern. At or near the central point of our civilization must come antithetical revelation, the turbulent child of the Altar.'

The womb analogy of 'Cavern' in this passage connects suggestively with its use in 'The Gyres'. There it is the subconscious areas of personality which give birth to the commands put upon the conscious intellect. Yeats, in the passage above, appends a curious footnote. While I am not certain that it adds much to the cavern metaphor, it nevertheless has a peripheral use in demonstrating how arbitrarily Yeats picked up material which became highly charged with symbolic meaning and spread out in ever-widening circles into the texture of his thought and work. 'I am thinking', he says, 'of two symbols found by Frobenius in Africa, the Cavern, symbol of the nations moving westwards, the Altar at the centre of radiating roads, symbol of the nations moving eastwards.' While, apparently insensitive to the

---

[3] I cannot resist the temptation to point out how Yeats repeats the triumph of 'A Coat':

'For there's more enterprise
In walking naked,'

in a poem written some thirty years later and with equal success.

naïveté of this attempt to describe the movements of cultures, Yeats puts forward his own position unambiguously, if unscientifically: 'I, upon the other hand, must think all civilizations equal at their best; every phase returns, therefore in some sense every civilization.' This belief, like many others Yeats held on allied subjects at this time, is taken over almost in its entirety from Flinders Petrie's *The Revolutions of Civilizations* and F. von Hügel's *The Mystical Element of Religion*.[4]

The deep subconscious impulses welling up from the 'cavern' check the denying intellect which has renounced the 'painted forms and boxes of make-up' sought in ancient tombs. The materials of the latter image are almost certainly derived from Yeats's early study of occult symbols as well as the cabalistic exercises and charts of the Hermetic students and Madame Blavatsky's theosophical group. Intuition or impulse contradicts the renouncing intellect with the imperative 'Rejoice!' This reading of the second stanza is substantiated by the heavy ironical intonation of 'What matter?' coming after the resolve to give up the fruitless sighs for an impossible past. The fact that the question is separated from 'not again' only by a semicolon, which does not effectively end-stop the line, shows that Yeats meant it as a mocking echo, an involuntary negation of the weak resolve.

[4] Petrie, the great nineteenth-century archaeologist, and von Hügel, the historian of mystical thought, shared some ideas, although whether the two influenced one another is neither within my interests nor my competency to ascertain. In any event, they apparently appealed to Yeats for similar reasons. In von Hügel, Yeats found an eruditely argued thesis regarding the impact of mystical experience on spiritual life. Von Hügel, as early as 1908, was trying to revive Kierkegaard. Yeats also found in von Hügel an attractively simple, if naïve scheme to account for the character of Western culture.

But it was von Hügel's conclusion which proved most congenial to Yeats for it squared with his own assessment. Von Hügel wrote that it was 'only through self-renunciation and suffering that the soul can win its true self, its abiding joy in union with the source of life . . . and the choice between two things alone: the noble pangs of spiritual childbirth, of painful joyous expansion and growth; and the shameful ache of spiritual death, of dreary contraction and decay.'

In Petrie's *The Revolutions of Civilizations* (1911), Yeats found a metaphor which he took over as a *principle* in his own description of the revolutions of civilizations. Petrie employs the concept behind the 'Great Year' of the ancients, but he is careful to point out that this is merely a metaphor based on the natural cycle of summer and winter which has come to stand for the decline and fall of civilizations. Being an archaeologist, Petrie takes sculpture as the test of the strength of a civilization, a concept which we see Yeats borrows in 'The Statues'.

One suspects that the most influential features of Petrie's thought for Yeats were his dread of democracy which he sees as 'the regular feature of decaying civilizations', and his belief that the condition of a civilization's continuance demands strife. 'There is no advance without strife.' Unlike Yeats, however, Petrie looks to the future with a great surge of inherited nineteenth-century optimism. The verse-play, 'A Full Moon in March', is interesting, among other reasons, for its reflection of some of Petrie's ideas. See, for example, the lines:

Great nations blossom above
A slave bows down to a slave.

'A greater, a more gracious time has gone' represents a conclusion Yeats had reached at as far back as 1909 when he had written in his diary that to oppose the new ill-breeding of Ireland, 'I can set up a secondary or interior personality, created out of the tradition of myself and this personality (alas, only possible to me in my writing) must be always gracious and simple. . .'. What qualities he attached to these adjectives is further intimated when he added 'A great lady is as simple as a good poet'.

In 'The Gyres' Yeats is in effect abandoning personal responsibility for making a reality of such graciousness '. . . . I sighed, but not again'; and putting all the intensity of his wilful old heart into the gyres, those principles of the revolutions of cultures which would restore from the sepulchre certain aspects of the past which he had always connected with 'graciousness'. But in the twenties, let us say, Yeats would have assigned more power to the men of action, the 'lovers of horses and of women', whom he still held dear. Now, he sees them in the service of the gyrating cones of history and as auxiliary forces which, together with these cyclic processes, will contrive a return to the conditions he requires for 'Unity of Being'.

Another mark of the subtlety of the Yeatsian vocabulary is to be seen in the use of 'noble' in this same stanza. An overworked adjective in nineteenth-century poetry, it is entirely unobjectionable here because used as a noun. In this archaic sense it operates as co-evalent with 'workman' and 'saint' and seems to restore an original moral lustre to the persons it denotes, a lustre which we should not so readily credit to the 'nobility'.

By the time we reach the 'What matter?' of the last stanza, the phrase has become so charged with scorn and derision that it forces an answer. In this truly apocalyptic passage Rocky Face is told that all the things he values will 'run on that unfashionable gyre again'. 'The dark betwixt the polecat and the owl' is the source from which the new-old order will spring.[5] It is typical of Yeats's method that he saw no contradiction between the 'irrational streams of blood' as defiling earth and man, and the same instinctual sources ('rich, dark nothing') as generating the new cycle of fulfilment.

It is the word 'unfashionable' in the last line of the poem which suggests both irony and self-criticism. For Yeats must have known that his mystical 'gyres' were 'unfashionable'—and in a double sense. They were intellectually unfashionable as an explanation of the movements of cultures; this particular gyre was politically unfashionable in a scientific, democratic society. For his motive, 'unfashionable' is a magnificent choice, the only sophisticated word in the whole poem, and by its prose quality setting the poem in time and robbing it a little of its gnomic intensity. Thus, it is really an expository short-cut and, while helpful, reduces rather than heightens the spontaneity

[5] See *A Vision* where Phase One is described as 'not being human'. See also the poem 'Phases of the Moon' for further elucidation of the 'ideas' of his passage.

of the prophecy. That this was a deliberately contrived effect I have no doubt. For Yeats would be the first to know that we have not now the ears with which to hear a 'pure' mantic intonation.

From *W. B. Yeats: The Tragic Phase. A Study of the Last Poems*, London: Routledge and Kegan Paul, 1951, pp. 95–108.

JOHN BAYLEY

The Coherence of Yeats's Poetry

So much detailed and authoritative criticism of Yeats's poetry has recently appeared that a further contribution might well appear unnecessary. We have had studies of his personality, his symbolic system, his mysticism, and his changes of style. Many of his poems have been carefully analysed, and their obscurities explained by reference to his multifarious interest in legend and magic, the Irish scene, painting, historical ideology. The influence of the French Symbolists, and of Swinburne and the poets of the *fin-de-siècle*, has been duly noted. But all this criticism, emphasizing as it does one or other of the aspects of Yeats's work, has an oddly fragmented quality. Disclaimers are frequent: critics who interpret his magic system are careful to insist that the excellence of his poetry is in no way dependent on it, and those who have commented on the peculiarity of his ideas, or analysed the progression of his thought, usually conclude that his greatness in some way lies outside them.

By implication, therefore, Yeats's achievement remains parcelled out under such heads as his style, his metrical and colloquial energy, and the aesthetic splendour of his great symbols such as Byzantium and the Tower. His vision as a whole, his world as a whole, is not taken seriously and not allowed as the real measure of his greatness. The unspoken critical verdict is that in Yeats's case the whole is not greater than the sum of its parts—that it is in fact a good deal smaller. And this is ironic, because Yeats was more consciously preoccupied than other romantic writers by the desire for a poetic vision that should be total, all-inclusive, while remaining outside any official system, religious or ideological—ways to live and think by which Yeats might dally with and draw upon, but which he always ended by insisting, 'are not my ways'. This refusal to commit himself is characteristic of an attitude which sought on the one hand to escape from the unworldly mind regions of the Symbolists, and on the other, not to become 'public' in the opprobrious sense of accepting the values and beliefs of the age and making poetry out of them. Yeats, like Wordsworth, determined to be a traveller whose tale was only of himself, but how was that self to be kept interesting, to be kept both apart from life and engaged in it? That, for Yeats, was the romantic poet's dilemma, and his whole development can best be seen as a series of brilliant and self-conscious expedients for solving it. The purpose and the will behind these expedients give a coherence and a vision to all the poetry, once we have understood them.

Crudely speaking, the criterion of romantic success is to imagine a world different from anyone else's. This may be done self-consciously, by a perpetual, strong-willed juggling with abstracts and events, as in the case of Yeats; or instinctively, by the natural cast of mind and imagination, as in the case of Walter de la Mare or—to take a very different example—Dylan Thomas. But all romantics are Robinson Crusoes, alone on a wide wide sea, and driven by 'le coeur Robinson' to produce their own version of reality. In his youthful experiences Wordsworth had perceived 'modes of being' which before him had hardly been conceived of as possessing independent significance and value, but he came eventually to accept and to live by beliefs of a much more conventional kind. The separation foreshadowed between the poetic apprehension and a process of coming to terms with life was one that haunted Yeats. And, paradoxically, he sees the way out in terms of becoming a complex personality instead of a simple one; if the self cannot always retain one poetry-giving vision before it, it must become many different selves. It must cultivate disciplines, attitudes, forms and models that it would not take to naturally, *personae* uncongenial to it—and all must be co-ordinated and carried through by the force of the poet's will. He blames Wordsworth for his singleness, remarking: 'if we cannot imagine ourselves as different from what we are, we cannot impose a discipline upon ourselves.' If his *raison d'être*, to create his own individual vision, is to endure, the romantic poet must submit to artificial disciplines and exercises which will enable him to 'embody reality' in his verse even if he does not perceive it in the world or by believing in any religion or ideology. 'For'—as Yeats puts it—

> though heart might find relief
> Did I become a Christian man and choose for my belief
> What seems most welcome in the tomb—play a predestined part[1]—

such a capitulation would be the end of him as a poet. Not that he cannot develop systems and ideologies of his own—Yeats spawned them like a salmon—but he must be at every moment prepared to abandon them or turn them inside out, and continue in a state of 'fruitful uncertainty'.

Keats's phrase is illuminating. For there is a sense, and a rather absurd sense to those to whom the attempt seems misguided, in which Yeats seems to be trying to achieve negative capability by numbers, to become 'a Proteus of the fire and flood' by means of a kind of athletic technique. If we think artificiality on this scale superbly distasteful, we cannot be in complete sympathy with Yeats's outlook. But if we understand its origins and the premises on which it rests,

[1] 'Vacillation'.

G

there is no reason why we should find it more distasteful than—
say—the attempts of Spenser, Sidney and their contemporaries to
create artificially a new English poetry. Full appreciation of Yeats is
hampered by preconceptions about the nature of poetry which are,
ironically enough, based on the very romantic ideals with which he is
so fundamentally in sympathy. We expect a great romantic poet to
exhibit an inclusive and individual vision; but we also expect this
to be in some way 'natural', to have developed spontaneously in the
context of his creative power, and to emerge like the leaves on the
tree. His *poetry*, we think, may be artificial, for poetry is after all a
formal art, but his *vision* must be spontaneous. But Yeats will not
admit this. His vision and his poetry are equally artificial, equally the
product of theory and the will, or, as he would have said, equally the
product of 'blood, imagination, intellect, running together'. In his
desire for the romantic wholeness of vision and poetic personality
Yeats is prepared to throw over the whole romantic conception of
the ideal, and the spontaneous overflow.

It follows from his idea of the inflexible wholeness of artificiality
that there must be nothing *outside* poetry which either causes it to
flow or prevents it. Abstract thought is dangerous, he sees; he deplores
his tendency to think in theories and abstractions, and he is humble
when the young James Joyce accuses him of generalizing, and of talking more like a man of letters than a poet. What is to be done? He
cannot submit to abstraction, but he will not banish it either, for that
would rob poetry of its inclusiveness. He must artificialize it, then:
he must marry the abstract attitude with the rhythmical one, so that
it becomes 'an *effect* of verse [italics mine], spoken by a man almost
rhythm-drunk, to give the apex of long-mounting thought'. Youth and
its fervours, the golden age of romantic inspiration, is to be particularly distrusted. He has seen too many of

> The best-endowed, the elect,
> All by their youth undone,
> All, all, by that inhuman
> Bitter glory wrecked.

He goes on:

> But I have straightened out
> Ruin, wreck, and wrack;
> I toiled long years and at length
> Came to so deep a thought
> I can summon back
> All their wholesome strength.

We do not hear what the 'great thought' was, and we do not want
to. The poem is not about it, but—as so often with Yeats's poems—
about his feelings on his art and what has gone into it, about his art

itself. The best artificial subject is the artistic process, and how this
process works upon

> Poet's imaginings
> And memories of love,
> Memories of the words of women.
> All those things whereof
> Man makes a superhuman
> Mirror-resembling dream.[2]

'A superhuman mirror-resembling dream.' The phrase goes a long
way towards summing up what Yeats thought that poetry should be.
And poetry should never be produced, Yeats feels, by some external
emotion which remains more powerful than the poetry itself. War
and the emotions it aroused, since these could not be artificialized and
remained outside the poet's grasp, were unsuitable. They could never
be fully comprehended in the 'blood, imagination and intellect'. We
may be distressed by his attitude to Wilfred Owen's poetry, which he
calls 'all blood, dirt, and sucked sugar-stick', but we have to admit
that according to his own philosophy Yeats could not have accepted
Owen. 'The poetry is in the pity'—Owen's poignantly accurate
description of how his verse was written would have made no sense
to Yeats. How could poetry reside in some large general emotion
outside the author's scope and control? How could the poetry be
anywhere outside the poet? It is an inflexible application of the
romantic egotism that the poet's universe must be purely his own.
War must be a factor in the poet's consciousness, not a public
emotion. Both the justice and the injustice of Yeats's claim can be
seen if we compare a verse of his with what are perhaps the finest
lines Owen wrote. The subject is a dead soldier.

> Whether his deeper sleep lie shaded by the shaking
> Of great wings, and the thoughts that hung the stars,
> High-pillowed on calm pillows of God's making
> Above these clouds, these rains, the sleets of lead,
> And these winds' scimitars;
> —Or whether yet his thin and sodden head
> Confuses more and more with the low mould,
> His hair being one with the grey grass
> And finished fields of autumns that are old. . . .
> Who knows? Who hopes? Who troubles? Let it pass.
> He sleeps. He sleeps less tremulous, less cold,
> Than we who must awake, and waking, say Alas![3]

The sentiment of pity here is so deep that it does appear to leave
the poetry behind, to submerge the critical faculty, and to blind the

[2] 'The Tower'.
[3] 'Asleep'.

reader to the inferior, Flecker-like image of 'the thoughts that hung
the stars' and to the precise and almost Shakespearean strangeness
of *Confuses,* and *finished fields.* There is something 'extra-poetic' in
the very implausibility of the picture suggested by the literary flavour
of the images in the first part, while those of the second come from
the heart of an experience. And the poem seems to transcend both
the good and the bad in it. The poet's indifference to the great question asked depends upon his being too deeply involved, not in the
poetry, but in the situation which has produced the poetry. It is not
an indifference, as Yeats's would be, contrived of set purpose in the
interests of the poem. We might put beside Owen a stanza from
Yeats's poem 'Nineteen Hundred and Nineteen'.

> Now days are dragon-ridden, the nightmare
> Rides upon sleep: a drunken soldiery
> Can leave the mother, murdered at her door,
> To crawl in her own blood, and go scot-free;
> The night can sweat with terror as before
> We pieced our thoughts into philosophy,
> And planned to bring the world under a rule,
> Who are but weasels fighting in a hole.

At first sight there seems to be, if not pity, at least a straightforward, 'non-poetic' indignation in these lines. But as we complete
our reading, we see that Yeats has subdued the image of the murdered
mother in the interests of his own vision of the times, which is at
once more withdrawn, more comprehensive, and more personal. The
very word *crawl,* joining up with the image in the last line, suggests some meaningless turbulence of animal suffering (comparable to
the images of such suffering in *King Lear* to which we are introduced
by Lear's desire 'to crawl unburdened towards death'). This is
contrasted with the rule of art and thought. Their coincidence in the
poet's mind, his ability to move from one to the other with comprehen-
sion but without emotion or regret, makes the vision peculiarly *his*:
past order and present anarchy both seem, for the moment, to exist
solely in order that Yeats may perceive how to fasten on to the contrast
and make poetry out of it.

The determination to be himself lies at the back of Yeats's famous
rejection of his early manner and of the conventional handling of Irish
Mythology. This kind of poetry is not his real self but only 'a coat',

> Covered with embroideries
> Out of old mythologies
> From heel to throat;
> But the fools caught it,
> Wore it in the world's eyes
> As though they'd wrought it.
> Song, let them take it,

For there's more enterprise
In walking naked.

The lines have often been quoted to illustrate his change of style,
but it is more important that they show his determination not to
draw any longer upon what had become a common stock of romantic
material. His vision must be his own; 'Walking naked' was being
Yeats, and this ability to disown old selves in his search for new tech-
niques of becoming a completely individual poetic self distinguishes
him from the other poets of the period even before his work had
begun to show its immense superiority over theirs. How completely
he identified himself with his poetry is seen in the verse he wrote after
receiving criticisms of the changes he had made in his early work.

They that hold that I do wrong
Whenever I remake a song
Should recollect what is at stake:
It is myself that I remake.

'How can we know the dancer from the dance?' he ends the poem
'Among School Children', and the image of the dancer, so rapt among
the many figures she makes that she seems a part of them, is one
of his formal symbols. This fanatical identification goes far to explain
how Yeats could continue to develop as he did, continuing to mirror
every fresh experience, physical and mental, that age brought him.
His inconsistency is a natural consequence of this development. High
passion and humorous earthy lust, bravado and pathos, public indignation and private self-mockery—all are compatible in the creating mind
that will not commit itself to anything but the poetry it can make of
them.

The comparison with Wilfred Owen has shown the limitations of the
process: poetry is life and life is poetry, and the very completeness
of the circle makes a kind of closed and insulated aesthetic. Although
there is nothing left out—indeed because there is nothing left out—
existence outside the circle seems for Yeats irrelevant, meaningless,
unimportant. There are no mysteries, no profundities outside, which
—as Owen obscurely felt about pity—poetry can touch but not trans-
mute; nothing which poetry must seek to become a part of, rather
than to absorb into itself. The doctrines of Symbolism, that logical
ending to romantic 'otherness', had had a deep influence upon Yeats.
Mallarmé had said: *Tout au monde existe pour aboutir à un livre.*
But for Mallarmé the world was the mind, the ultimate romantic
region in which poetry had its genesis and being. Yeats's self-
appointed task was to bring this Symbolist absolutism back to the
world of action and event, to make the outer world its province. But
the same uncompromising theory, the world for art's sake, underlies
its purpose. 'Words alone are certain good', he echoes Mallarmé in
one of his earliest poems, and the same principle dominated him to

the end. The influence of Symbolism was strengthened by that of Pater and the English aesthetes, and Yeats was the one disciple who was both serious and successful enough to give meaning to the famous passage about 'burning always with a hard gem-like flame': in the context of his mature manner the phrase acquires point. Of his associations with Arthur Symons, Yeats records that 'we always discussed life at its most intense moment'. Matthew Arnold had called religion 'morality touched by emotion': the goal of aesthetic behaviour was short and intense periods of emotion untouched by morality.

Compared with this conception of the artist, the influence of the actual theory of the Symbol on Yeats's work is comparatively unimportant. It exercises nothing like such a strong effect on the nature of the poetry as does the aesthetic background of late Romanticism. Yeats, as we have said, brings Romanticism back to earth, but he pays the price of making himself and his poetry the measure of all things. So, it may be argued, do all romantic poets, but never before with Yeats's self-conscious deliberation. Towards other poets and their experiences he maintained a careful policy of exclusion or non-comprehension. 'It may be a way', he would reiterate, 'but it is not my way'. The paradox of his later years is that though he followed keenly the course of politics and literary fashion, and read Spengler, Jung, Russell and other thinkers, he remained an isolated figure, whose vision, though it drew on these materials, remained too completely his own to seem anything but outlandish, reactionary and uncongenial to the younger writers. 'Like Balzac', he wrote in a letter, 'I know no one who shares the premises from which I work'. T. S. Eliot, reviewing *The Cutting of an Agate* in *The Athenaeum*, adopts a tone of extreme disapproval, and speaks of Yeats's vision as 'egotistic and crude'. Eliot, we remember, was already seeking to commit himself to values which could not be subdued into the aesthetic vision of the individual. W. H. Auden, writing in *The Kenyon Review*, remarked that Yeats's rhythm and the controversial power of his poetry had had tremendous influence, but his vision, none. While agreeing with Auden's tribute to the influence of Yeats's style, we may wonder whether the latter's view of what the poet should be has really had so little effect. Auden himself goes on to say that Yeats turned the occasional poem into a *genre* of real importance: and he implies that this was done by Yeats's ability to endow his friends, his family and house and daily life with such an urgent and sumptuous poetic existence. The small doings of his friends—Mrs French and her butler, Henry Middleton and his quiet house in a Sligo suburb—become as incalculably significant as the deeds of epic heroes. 'All the Olympians, a thing never known again.' Simply by virtue of the relationship, Yeats's grandfather joins the 'half legendary men', the company of Pearse and Cuchulain, Parnell and Casement. Nor is there anything laughable in this association: Yeats's total absence of self-consciousness, the grandeur of his insulation, if one may so call it, makes his valuation of these personalities and happenings completely convincing. Now Auden's own poetic vision, where it is most effective and compelling, seems to owe much to Yeats's example in this respect. As we shall see, Auden succeeds just as effectively as Yeats in endowing the apparent trivialities of life with a mysterious significance, a kind of esoteric harmony, and his vision is just as uncommitted to an allegiance *outside its own existence as poetry* as is Yeats's own. This particular romantic survival, in fact, depends on the poet's success in creating a world constructed of simple recognizable materials—friends, houses, careers, cars, gasometers, the Communist Party—but transformed by a fine conspiracy of style and manner into something *eo ipso,* an aesthetic world in which, as Auden puts it, 'what delights us is just that it neither is nor could possibly become one in which we could breathe or behave'.

From 'W. B. Yeats', *The Romantic Survival: A Study in Poetic Evolution,* London: Constable, 1957, pp. 77–126 (81–92).

EDWARD ENGELBERG

The Nature of Yeats's Symbols

To turn to 'Magic' is, I think, a legitimate digression; the essay is
dated 1901, the year following the essay on the symbolism of poetry,
but it is safe to assume that the two pieces are nearly contempor-
aneous. In 'Magic' Yeats states his three famous beliefs:

(1) That the borders of our mind are ever shifting, and that many
    minds can flow into one another ... and create or reveal a
    single mind, a single energy.
(2) That the borders of our memories are as shifting, and that
    our memories are a part of one great memory, the memory of
    Nature herself.
(3) That this great mind and great memory can be evoked by
    symbols.

For present purposes, the second and third beliefs have the greatest
relevance. Individual memories are saved from an egoistic or ego-
centric point of view when they become part of the 'great memory'
—something achievable, Yeats felt, only by the best poets. He had
tried, he confesses in 'Magic', to make distinctions between 'inherent
symbols and arbitrary symbols', symbols arising out of a received
tradition or seemingly invented arbitrarily by the poet; but the
distinction, he says, came 'to mean little or nothing'.[1] (It is worth
noting in passing, however, that in 'Prometheus Unbound', 1932, Yeats
returned to the distinction, calling Shelley's symbols 'arbitrary' and
saying of him: 'his system of thought was constructed by his logical
faculty ... not a symbolical revelation received'.[2]) Ultimately what
the poet did with his symbols determined their power. 'Whether their
power has arisen out of themselves, or whether it has an arbitrary
origin, matters little, for they act ... because the great memory associates them with certain events and moods and persons.'[3]
  To return to the essay on Symbolism:

'If I watch a rushy pool in the moonlight, my emotion at its beauty
is mixed with memories of the man that I have seen ploughing by
its margin, or of the lovers I saw there a night ago....'

This, then, is the 'emotional symbol' and what Yeats would call at

[1] 'Magic', *Essays and Introductions*, pp. 33, 60.
[2] 'Prometheus Unbound', ibid., p. 421.
[3] 'Magic', ibid., p. 60.

one time the 'arbitrary' symbol, for it depends primarily on personal associations.

> '... but if I look at the moon herself and remember any of her ancient names and meanings, I move among divine people, and things that have shaken off our mortality, the tower of ivory, the queen of waters, the shining stag among enchanted woods...'[4]

And here is the 'intellectual symbol' evoking 'ideas mingled with emotion', joining the reader to the 'procession', making him respond to a symbol that is 'inherent' (as distinct from 'arbitrary'). Note that Yeats says, 'if I *look* at the moon herself', not if I *think* of her: looking precedes thinking; the symbol is its own starting point, not the end but the beginning of the process.

Whether in practice Yeats was a Symbolist poet (in the Blakean sense) or a *symboliste* poet has been in dispute ever since Edmund Wilson confidently placed Yeats among the latter in *Axel's Castle*. The question is not likely to be decided to everyone's satisfaction. It has often been argued that Yeats was not a *symboliste* poet because he got his doctrines second hand from Arthur Symons and could read French only slowly and with great difficulty. This is a pretty thin argument; apply it more generally, and you deprive Yeats of an understanding of all foreign literatures, since he was a poor reader of any language except his own. All the evidence indicates that Yeats's understanding of *symbolisme* was neither shallow nor haphazard; if he departed from these doctrines he did not do so out of ignorance of what he was departing from and his own goals were very clearly set. A tentative distinction between Yeats's conception of symbol and that of the *symbolistes* is possible, though I would be careful to point out that the distinction does not hold either for all of Yeats's poetry or for all of the poetry of *symbolisme*—luckily, I would add, since no great poets fit intellectual distinctions rigidly. Yet I do think it is possible to say that for the *symboliste* poet, let us say Baudelaire, the symbol is the end product, not the starting point. So Baudelaire's Paris (like Eliot's London) is his starting point, and often a very realistically rendered one; it is only gradually that the city itself becomes the City, and the City in turn something else—a hospital full of sick people, a hell, a house of prostitution. Baudelaire is interested primarily in his symbol, not that which goes into its making; the world is used to evoke the symbol. Yeats, I think, came to work in the opposite direction: he would use the symbol to evoke the world, and his interest, ultimately, was less in the symbol than in the things evoked. Hence, of course, his great desire to achieve 'multitude'. For Yeats the symbol became a true metaphor which evoked the world in terms of itself, and I have already quoted in the preceding chapter the notion of 'correspondences' which Yeats out-

---

[4] 'The Symbolism of Poetry', ibid., pp. 198–199.

lined to his father and which differs considerably from Baudelaire's *correspondances*. It is clear from the excerpts quoted above that the symbol—say, the moon or the rushy pool—does not always evoke a multitude that is realistic or worldly, using those words in their simplest meaning: one thinks either of personal associations or of ancient mythological and folklore traditions. But in either case the mind expands from the symbol, whether it be rushy pool or moon, and that symbol is, in both cases, a 'real' object.

The best example that comes to mind from Yeats's poems is Sato's sword, and the use Yeats makes of it in 'A Dialogue of Self and Soul':

> The consecrated blade upon my knees
> Is Sato's ancient blade, still as it was,
> Still razor-keen, still like a looking-glass
> Unspotted by the centuries;
> That flowering, silken, old embroidery, torn
> From some court-lady's dress and round
> The wooden scabbard bound and wound,
> Can, tattered, still protect, faded adorn.

Yeats says that the sword and the embroidery are his 'emblems' of day set against the emblem of night, the tower, another real object since it is his own tower he is writing about. So both sword and tower are real objects from which Yeats begins; and he begins with these objects already established as his symbols. The objective, therefore, is not to make the real sword or the real tower into symbols, but to let the symbols work upon the imagination so as to evoke 'love and war'—the five hundred years which is the life of the blade itself, the woman from whom, perhaps in some violent struggle, the embroidery was torn, the tumultuous and multitudinous associations that are both history in the abstract and the symbol's own history (of which I spoke earlier). T. Sturge Moore designed the bookplate for Yeats's volume *The Tower*, and in a letter of instructions from Yeats, in 1927, there is a passage relevant to our present discussion: 'I need not make any suggestions, except that the Tower should not be too unlike the real object, or rather that it should suggest the real object. I like to think of that building as a permanent symbol of my work plainly visible to the passer-by.' Indeed, as early as 1908 (in a Note to *The Wind among the Reeds* in the *Collected Works*), Yeats had confessed the weakness of an over-indulgence in symbols for their own sake; these in turn required 'lengthy notes' to clarify what he felt to be a 'reckless obscurity'. But into these notes he had, he admits, put 'more wilful phantasy than I now think admirable. . . .' He would from now on stay closer to 'the real object'.[5]

---

[5] Ursula Bridge (ed.), *W. B. Yeats and T. Sturge Moore: Their Correspondence*, p. 114; *Variorum Edition*, p. 800.

When Rimbaud takes a 'blade' as his symbol in 'Honte' he works the matter quite differently from the manner in which Yeats treated his 'consecrated blade':

Tant que la lame n'aura
Pas coupé cette cervelle,
Ce paquet blanc, vert et gras,
A vapeur jamais nouvelle...

Rimbaud's blade is an unspecified object, real only in the sense that it is an object taken from the real world. Like Yeats, Rimbaud begins with the object, but the 'symbolic' quality of the blade becomes clear only as the poem progresses, and as we get farther away from its concrete associations and closer to what Rimbaud wants us to associate with it:

(Ah! Lui, devrait couper son
Nez, sa lèvre, ses oreilles,
Son ventre! et faire abandon
De ses jambes! ô merveille!)

Mais, non; vrai, je crois que tant
Que pour sa tête la lame,
Que les cailloux pour son flanc,
Que pour ses boyaux la flamme...

Rimbaud's blade is not quite the same as Baudelaire's Paris, since Baudelaire was a greater master of rendering the realistic detail before moving on to its symbolic implications. But both Rimbaud and Baudelaire desire effects that terminate in the symbol; Yeats the effects that are generated by it—toward associations that cannot properly be called symbolic any more, except as we call love, war, violence, courtly ladies, 'symbolic' abstractions, poetic short-cuts, allusions.

One might go on making comparisons; for instance, one could take Yeats's symbol of the swan in 'The Wild Swans at Coole' and set it against Baudelaire's use of the swan in 'Le Cygne' and arrive at a similar distinction; but further comparisons would lead us too far afield from the present subject. I have suggested the difference in treatment, not because I think it operates unfailingly, but because it contains an essential truth worth stating: while *symbolisme* moved toward a coalescing symbol, Yeats moved away from an exfoliating one.

From *The Vast Design: Patterns in W. B. Yeats's Aesthetic*, University of Toronto Press, 1964, pp. 108–12.

RICHARD ELLMANN

Yeats and Auden:
An Imaginary Conversation

Their views constitute a running dialogue, formulated by them more or less in this way:

YEATS: I believe in the poet's evocation of disembodied powers which, assuming form through the mind, effect changes in the world. The proper metaphor for poetry is magic.[1]

AUDEN: Poetry is not magic. Insofar as it has an ulterior purpose, this is, by telling the truth, to disenchant and disintoxicate.[2]

YEATS: Truth is the dramatic expression of the highest man, of the poet as hero.[3]

AUDEN: The poet no longer fancies himself a hero; he is an explorer of possibility.[4]

YEATS: Say impossibility rather.

AUDEN: All that is passé with the romantic movement, thank God. Crying has gone out and the cold bath has come in.[5]

YEATS: The whale is extinct and the little fish lie gasping on the strand.[6]

AUDEN: The artist no longer wanders about in exile, he builds irrigation ditches like Faust in his old age, he votes in elections.[7]

YEATS: The artist has much more in common with the flood than with irrigation. He breaks out of every social dam or political enclosure.

AUDEN: You belong to the school of Mallarmé; you think of yourself as a god who creates the subjective universe out of nothing.[8]

YEATS: You belong to the school of Locke; you split the world into fragments and then worship the cutting edge.[9]

[1] 'Magic', *Essays and Introductions*, p. 28, and 'The Symbolism of Poetry', ibid., pp. 158–59.

[2] *The Dyer's Hand*, p. 27.

[3] Yeats and Edwin John Ellis, *The Works of William Blake*, London, 1893, V. I, p. 241; Ellmann, *Yeats: The Man and The Masks*, p. 6.

[4] *The Enchafèd Flood*, New York, 1950, p. 152.

[5] Auden and Macneice, *Letters from Iceland*, p. 25.

[6] 'A General Introduction for My Work', *Essays and Introductions*, pp. 525–26; and his poem, 'The Three Movements'.

[7] *The Enchafèd Flood*, p. 153; cf. his view of Shakespeare in *The Dyer's Hand*, pp. 182–90.

[8] *The Dyer's Hand*, p. 76.

[9] 'Fragments', and his descriptions of phases 23 and 24 in *A Vision*.

AUDEN: Your world is a chimera.
YEATS: Yours is an urban renewal project.

Before the poets become too heated, perhaps we may try to placate them a little. Yeats is apt to say more than he means, Auden to say less. Yeats regarded himself as a romantic—a school which, like Eliot, Auden professes to detest; yet the bold positions which Yeats shares with romantic poets appear in his verse often with a modern wariness and qualification. They are outposts flung up with a keen sense of imperilment. Auden regards himself as a classicist, yet that term implies a much more settled manner and matter than his work displays. He may be described more profitably as an anti-romantic within the romantic tradition. In a recent poem he declares that he would have liked to sing 'In the old grand manner/Out of a resonant heart,' but that he has been forced by the debasement of words and values to adopt 'the wry, the sotto-voce,/Ironic and monochrome'. It is not like Auden to blame the age for his style, and in fact from the start he has clearly preferred to reject the idealization of art and manner that accompanies it. Yet at moments he has not been adamant. In *The Sea and the Mirror* Prospero asks Ariel to show in his mirror what Nature is for ever, and when he does so, says, 'one peep... will be quiet enough'. But if the mirror of art can show even one peep at nature in its eternal form, then it must be more powerful than he customarily allows. In his last prose book, *The Dyer's Hand*, Auden for the first time repeatedly emphasizes that poetry is a rite, surrounded with awe. Instead of limiting it to an engaging but futile game, he has it subtly remaking the relations of the sacred and the profane, perhaps also of the real and the unreal, of the one and the many. This is about as much as Yeats would claim. At another door, Auden's anti-mythological attitude would seem to be a myth of its own, a belittlement of traditional glories only to make a reduced but very solid residual claim, like stripping a Victorian house of its ginger-bread in order to display its solidity.

At least once in later poems Yeats and Auden converge on the same subject. This is a moment of lay sanctity experienced in a restaurant. Auden is full of casual and seemingly gratuitous detail:

IN SCHRAFFT'S

Having finished the Blue-plate Special
And reached the coffee stage,
Stirring her cup she sat,
A somewhat shapeless figure
Of indeterminate age
In an undistinguished hat.

When she lifted her eyes it was plain
That our globular future,

Our international rout
Of sin and apparatus
And dying men galore,
Was not being bothered about.

Which of the seven heavens
Was responsible her smile
Wouldn't be sure but attested
That, whoever it was, a god
Worth kneeling-to for a while
Had tabernacled and rested.

Yeats's poem on a similar theme comes in the series called 'Vacillation':

My fiftieth year had come and gone,
I sat, a solitary man,
In a crowded London shop,
An open book and empty cup
On the marble table-top.

While on the shop and street I gazed
My body of a sudden blazed;
And twenty minutes more or less
It seemed, so great my happiness,
That I was blessèd and could bless.

Auden carries the commonplaceness of the shop a little further than
Yeats, and he limits the intensity of the experience described.
Characteristically the latter is not his own, but that of someone
'shapeless' he doesn't know, of indeterminate age, who wears an undistinguished hat, as if she were describable only in negative terms.
The religious imagery is operated differently in the two poems: it
serves Yeats to describe a blasphemous encroachment of the human
upon the divine, while in Auden an earthier god makes his positive
incursion upon the human, an incursion less weighty, less implicat-
ing, more sanguine. Auden's metaphor is genuinely religious and yet
ironically reduced: food in the tabernacle of the belly constitutes a
certain good.

The movement has been from candid intensity to intense candour.
Auden's offhand, unassuming tone, his disinfected vocabulary, take on
some of their authority by disavowing what in Yeats is so assuming,
so infected. As Proust remarks, 'A powerful idea communicates some
of its strength to him who challenges it.' If Yeats, and poets like
him, had not already extolled the poem as a terrestrial paradise, a
fragment of Eden, a symbol of heaven, Auden might have felt less
disposed to belittle it as a 'verbal contraption'.[10] These terms are not

10 *The Dyer's Hand*, p. 50.

mutually exclusive: they represent different kinds of assertion and defiance at different moments. Yeats with overstatement, and Auden with understatement, circle furtively toward each other, caught in the same galactic system.

From *Eminent Domain: Yeats among Wilde, Joyce, Pound, Eliot and Auden*, New York: Oxford University Press, 1967, pp. 122–26.

LAURENCE LERNER

Yeats's Poetic World

When you read Yeats's poetry, purely as poetry, what is it about?
Is it about anything coherent? Did he write a lot of individual
poems merely, or did he create a poetic world?

I am sure he did: as coherent and valuable a world as any modern
poet. It's true that his poems occasionally contradict one another:
total consistency is an appalling virtue. In particular, he varies between the joyous view that 'everything we look upon is blest', and the
bleak view that love is a consolation in a world

> [Where] the crime of being born
> Blackens all our lot.

But a lot of what may look like inconsistency is simply the evidence
of the ceaseless dialogue that he held with himself. More than once
he held the dialogue out loud and explicitly, most notably in his
'Dialogue of Self and Soul'. I believe that this poem lies in the very
centre of Yeats's work. If I was forced to name his best single poem
I'd be tempted to choose it; if I had to name the most typical of his
best poems, the one with most repercussions in his other work,
I'd choose it without hesitation. It is in two parts, and I'd like to read
the first with you (the dialogue proper) as carefully as time permits.

The Soul begins, exhorting to withdrawal, solitude, study (study of
Plotinus, perhaps, or of *A Vision*):

> I summon to the winding ancient stair;
> Set all your mind upon the steep ascent,
> Upon the broken, crumbling battlement,
> Upon the breathless, starlit air,
> Upon the star that marks the hidden pole;
> Fix every wandering thought upon
> That quarter where all thought is done:
> Who can distinguish darkness from the soul?

'Wandering' had been a favourite romantic adjective of the early, undisciplined Yeats, where hair strays and stars wander the sky. Now
such fancies are to be kept sternly in order: *set all your mind* upon
the steep ascent. Only the last line of the stanza seems puzzling:
'Who can distinguish darkness from the soul?' It suggests to us how
total is the austerity, the withdrawal from common life, that is being

urged; and by the end of the poem its significance will have become clearer.

Then comes one of those touches of genius that never fail Yeats. The Self does not even answer. So absorbed is the Self in living, so uninterested in withdrawal and in pure thought, that it stares at the blade on its knees, too fascinated to do more than murmur to itself:

> The consecrated blade upon my knees
> Is Sato's ancient blade, still as it was,
> Still razor-keen, still like a looking glass
> Unspotted by the centuries;
> That flowering, silken old embroidery, torn
> From some court-lady's dress and round
> The wooden scabbard bound and wound,
> Can, tattered, still protect, faded adorn.

The Self does not even say that the sword is a symbol: the Soul does that, in a moment. It was, as a matter of fact, a real sword, given to Yeats by a Japanese admirer; and the intricate, meditative lines about it make it seem real to us, and the memories real that it calls up.

Soul speaks again:

> Why should the imagination of a man
> Long past his prime remember things that are
> Emblematical of love and war?
> Think of ancestral night that can,
> If but imagination scorn the earth
> And intellect its wandering
> To this and that and t'other thing,
> Deliver from the crime of death and birth.

Perhaps Soul's tone is pitying as well as scornful in the beginning, shaking his head sadly as he says 'Why should the imagination of a man...' But scorn imposes itself, and the contemptuous word 'wandering' appears again, this time more contemptuously still. Then in the last line, with its fierce opening verb like a loud chord, scorn transforms itself to dignity and massive movement:

> Deliver from the crime of death and birth.

The Self is still staring at the sword:

> Montashigi, third of his family, fashioned it
> Five hundred years ago, about it lie
> Flowers from I know not what embroidery—
> Heart's purple, and all these I set
> For emblems of the day against the tower
> Emblematical of the night,
> And claim as by a soldier's right
> A charter to commit the crime once more.

H

I picture the Self looking slowly up during this stanza, as his lines slowly turn into a reply to the Soul: looking up and perhaps raising the sword as he announces, with a completely decisive rhythm.

> and all these I set
> For emblems of the day against the tower.

Taking over the Soul's metaphor of a crime, Self glories in it: he is as firm and as fierce as Soul was in the last stanza. Of course he will go on committing the crime: for

> Over the blackened earth
> The old troops parade.

And then, in its final proud verse, the Soul announces its own defeat. Where does its winding stair lead to? To a state of contemplation in which the senses will be suspended, personality will no longer exist:

> Such fullness in that quarter overflows
> And falls into the basin of the mind
> That man is stricken deaf and dumb and blind,
> For intellect no longer knows
> *Is* from the *Ought*, or *Knower* from the *Known*—
> That is to say, ascends to Heaven;
> Only the dead can be forgiven;
> But when I think of that my tongue's a stone.

Why does the Soul feel itself undone by the consummation it seeks? I suppose because it is not offering a religious dogma or religious hope. Detached from the body, the Soul may have no existence, or none worth having: so the path of withdrawal, the ascent to the tower, is one which you destroy yourself by following. When the Soul has ascended to Heaven, no one can distinguish it from darkness.

Why is this such a great poem? For one thing, because neither of the speakers is a puppet. The Soul was not put up simply to be knocked down, it offers what Yeats had given many years of his life to. If you read the essays that Yeats collected under the title *The Cutting of an Agate*, you can see the theme of this dialogue beginning to take shape. You can see him losing some of his old confidence in essences, in 'mysterious wisdom won by toil', and gaining a new wish for a 'delight in the whole man—blood, imagination, intellect, running together'. This is a contrast that runs right through the later Yeats, and takes many forms. It is the contrast between the musician and the orator, between 'the way of the bird until common eyes have lost us' and that of the market cart, between the learned man and the girl who goes to school to her mirror only, between the Soul and the Self. Partly, it is the contrast between the Bishop and Crazy Jane. The Self represents the totality of living, accepts 'the frog-spawn of a blind man's ditch'; the Soul chooses—abstracts—from life one thing, usually one intellectual thing, and pursues that only. What the Soul stands for we may therefore name abstraction.

This theme, of abstraction versus the fullness of living, ties in very naturally with the great theme of the later Yeats, his hatred of old age. Here is the opening section of *The Tower*:

> What shall I do with this absurdity—
> O heart, O troubled heart—this caricature,
> Decrepit age that has been tied to me
> As to a dog's tail?
>   Never had I more
> Excited, passionate, fantastical
> Imagination, nor an ear and eye
> That more expected the impossible—
> No, not in boyhood when with rod and fly,
> Or the humbler worm, I climbed Ben Bulben's back
> And had the livelong summer day to spend.
> It seems that I must bid the Muse go pack,
> Choose Plato and Plotinus for a friend
> Until imagination, ear and eye,
> Can be content with argument and deal
> In abstract things; or be derided by
> A sort of battered kettle at the heel.

The contrast here is between philosophy and fishing. Philosophy is done sitting at a desk; it is done with the intellect only; it is abstract. Fishing is a bodily activity, it is done by the whole man, it is done by young men, the young men of the third section of the poem:

> I leave both faith and pride
> To young upstanding men
> Climbing the mountain-side,
> That under bursting dawn
> They may drop a fly.

Yeats is a poet. Poetry is like philosophy in that it is a 'sedentary trade'; but it is also like fishing, for it is not abstract, it demands the whole man. But fishing is for the young, and the bitterness of this verse results from the conflict between what the poet wants and what would be appropriate to his age. It is this which gives such withering force to the image of the kettle when it reappears at the end, or such contempt to

> It seems that I must bid the Muse go pack,
> Choose Plato and Plotinus for a friend

(and how fortunate for Yeats that these two symbols of abstract thought begin with such a scornfully plosive sound as pl). What Troilus said of love, Yeats is here saying of age:

> 'This is the monstruosity in love, lady, that the will is infinite and the execution confined, that the desire is boundless and the act a slave to limit.'

Proudly and querulously Yeats says, over and over, that he will not accept his limits, that he will not give up the Muse, his lust, the boundlessness of his desire: he will not be an old scarecrow, a 'tattered coat upon a stick'.

There are other forms of abstraction besides study. To abstract is to take one thing only from life's complexity:

> Hearts with one purpose alone
> Through summer and winter seem
> Enchanted to a stone
> To trouble the living stream.

These are the hearts of the men of 1916, the leaders of the Easter Rising, who wrung a reluctant tribute from Yeats—his poem 'Easter 1916'. This poem tells how the men were transformed under the spell of violence, how they 'resigned their parts in the casual comedy' of everyday living, how a terrible beauty was born, a beauty that the poem celebrates. But in the middle of this hymn Yeats put a section that tells of the price they paid for their greatness. It is by far the best thing in the poem:

> Hearts with one purpose alone
> Through summer and winter seem
> Enchanted to a stone
> To trouble the living stream.
> The horse that comes from the road,
> The rider, the birds that range
> From cloud to tumbling cloud,
> Minute by minute they change;
> A shadow of cloud on the stream
> Changes minute by minute;
> A horse-hoof slides on the brim,
> And a horse plashes within it;
> The long-legged moorhens dive,
> And hens to moor-cocks call;
> Minute by minute they live:
> The stone's in the midst of all.

The stone is the symbol of the dedicated man, the man who sacrifices himself for political action and by his narrowness, his intensity, becomes 'a bitter, an abstract thing'. Even in this poem, the finest tribute that Yeats ever paid such men, he puts a picture of their limitations right in the centre: the stone is surrounded by the restlessness and variety of life. Nothing in 'Easter 1916' is so moving as this varied and subtle evocation of change, movement, and process, the rhythms and the rhymes shifting delicately to mirror the elusive life that washes against the stone. And when the section is over, the next, before moving to its conclusion of praise, lingers a moment to remind us bluntly how very limiting it is to call something a stone.

> Too long a sacrifice
> Can make a stone of the heart.

The stone ceases to be an image and becomes a mere idiom, so that there shall be no mistake.

But there is one form of abstraction that Yeats does defend: this is Art. Art too is out of living, it too is something frozen, something motionless, even (like the golden nightingale Yeats loved to refer to) something dead. But when the artist abstracts, he does so on a paradoxical principle: he is in search of just that essence which makes life full, rich, and changing. He seeks the very quality that Plato and Plotinus miss. This, I take it, is the theme of 'Sailing to Byzantium' (Yeats's 'Ode on a Grecian Urn'). Because he is old he must withdraw from nature, from the mackerel-crowded seas, from the welter of living that belongs to the young. It is now the turn of Soul: but in this poem Soul has a new function—not to climb the winding stair, but to sing. Its function now is to celebrate the Self. The figures on Keats's Grecian Urn were likewise frozen in a moment of change, and remain as permanent symbols of the most transient thing we know, youthful love. This underlying paradox gives such power to Keats's cry 'More happy love . . .

> . . . For ever panting and for ever young'

and to Yeats's golden nightingale, that has been gathered 'into the artifice of eternity', and yet sings

> Of what is past, or passing, or to come.

'Sailing to Byzantium' is a poem about art. Yeats wrote poem after poem in praise of art, and some of them are his finest. The very first poem in his first volume says 'words alone are certain good'; and though he learned to understand more and more fully what this meant, and what difficulties it implied, he never forsook the theme, or ceased to believe in words. In old age he praised art as the one form of abstraction that did not involve a rejection of the salmon-falls, the young men fishing, the pride like that of the morn. And all through his life he praised it for another reason that widens beyond a theory of art, and becomes a philosophy of living.

Let us divide theories of art, crudely, into two: those that stress the artistic experience itself, and those that stress its consequences.

If you value art because it brings wisdom and understanding, because it broadens the sympathies and stimulates the imagination, because it leads to the love of God, or the dictatorship of the proletariat, or a sharpening of the moral sensibilities, your theory of art can, in general, be called didactic. If, on the other hand, you value it because the actual experience of hearing the Ninth Symphony or reading the Odes of Keats is uniquely precious, and would be worth having even if it left no trace, even if you dropped down dead the next moment, if you dislike talk about the moral and social importance of art because that seems to come from those to whom the poems themselves do not matter enough, then your theory of art can, in general, be called aesthetic. Crude as this distinction is, it is not too crude for Yeats: for all his life he belonged quite firmly to the second camp. He was always impatient of attempts to put art to the service of something else; and because it is mainly the early Yeats we think of as an aesthete, I will illustrate with one of his last poems the first part of 'Lapis Lazuli':

> I have heard that hysterical women say
> They are sick of the palette and fiddle-bow,
> Of poets that are always gay,
> For everybody knows or else should know
> That if nothing drastic is done
> Aeroplane and Zeppelin will come out,
> Pitch like King Billy bomb-balls in
> Until the town lie beaten flat.
>
> All perform their tragic play,
> There struts Hamlet, there is Lear,
> That's Ophelia, that Cordelia;
> Yet they, should the last scene be there,
> The great stage curtain about to drop,
> If worthy their prominent part in the play,
> Do not break up their lines to weep.
> They know that Hamlet and Lear are gay;
> Gaiety transfiguring all that dread.
> All men have aimed at, found and lost;
> Black out; Heaven blazing into the head:
> Tragedy wrought to its uttermost.
> Though Hamlet rambles and Lear rages
> And all the drop-scenes drop at once
> Upon a hundred thousand stages,
> It cannot grow by an inch or an ounce.

This poem was written in the thirties, the great decade of political art; and I take it that the hysterical women of the first stanza are those for whom art is a luxury which, at times like these, must yield to politics: because the world is in a mess, we shall have no more poems, or at any rate none that do not aim to cure the mess.

Yeats was never one to deny that the world was in a mess: just before this poem comes 'The Gyres', with its terrible vision of how 'irrational streams of blood are staining earth'. What he denied was that art should aim to cure it. Art was not to be beautiful by ignoring suffering and turning its back on the real world: that had been the fault of his early poetry. But, having faced that world, it was to use it as material for tragedy. The artist should feel the troubles of his time as intensely as the actor must feel the sufferings of Lear; but if he feels them with an intensity that deflects him into a didactic purpose, he is like an actor who 'breaks up his lines to weep'. The poet builds his poem out of his feeling of compassion and urgency, but he does not sacrifice the poem to them. To make the point Yeats chose the most tendentious word he could to describe the experience of watching, or creating, a tragedy; and to shock the hysterical women, he called it gaiety. The true artist, worthy of his part, the true musician, of the 'accomplished fingers', do not run away from the mess the world is in, but they do turn it into a beauty that is gay. Many years before he had made the same point even more wildly, through the mouth of one of his many personae, Tom O'Roughley. Tom is talking of personal, not public sorrow, and so perhaps shocks us even more:

And if my dearest friend were dead
I'd dance a measure on his grave

(which was just what Yeats was doing, in that volume, in the very next poem in fact, to his friend Robert Gregory).

'Lapis Lazuli' states, then, that art offers an experience to be taken for its own sake only: that out of tragedy comes tragic joy. It is not only art that offers this. I suggested that this was a theory of art that widens into a way of living. To lose oneself in an experience so full that one no longer cares about the consequences is to live as fully as possible: to respond in this way to art, is a type of responding in such a way to all experience. I will therefore quote, as a parallel to 'Lapis Lazuli', a poem that is not about art at all; and I will end with this poem, for the very good reason that my time is up. I am glad to end on this theme, and on this poem. On this theme, because on the whole I am not of Yeats's camp on this matter. I believe in literature that does care about its consequences, and my admiration for those poems that state Yeats's aesthetic view is therefore wrung from me by the sheer splendour of the poems themselves. To confess to this admiration is, to me, the finest tribute I can pay Yeats the poet; and I can see that it is, in a sense though not a fatal sense, to yield to his position. And I am glad to end with this poem—'An Irish Airman foresees his Death'—for a whole lot of reasons. It was written near the middle of Yeats's career, and it resembles both his early and his late work: it is therefore an illustration of what I have been assuming through most of this talk, the continuity between the early and the late Yeats. It describes a delight that has many parallels, among them the pleasure I take in Yeats's poetry. And—if I may finish on the note of simple praise on which I began—it is one of my favourite poems:

I know that I shall meet my fate
Somewhere among the clouds above;
Those that I fight I do not hate,
Those that I guard I do not love;
My country is Kiltartan Cross,
My countrymen Kiltartan's poor,
No likely end could bring them loss
Or leave them happier than before.
Nor law, nor duty bade me fight,
Nor public men, nor cheering crowds,
A lonely impulse of delight
Drove to this tumult in the clouds;
I balanced all, brought all to mind,
The years to come seemed waste of breath,
A waste of breath the years behind
In balance with this life, this death.

From 'W. B. Yeats: Poet and Crank', *Proceedings of the British Academy*, vol. XLIX, 1963 (O.U.P., 1964), pp. 49–67, (59–67).

Select Bibliography

TEXTS:

EDITIONS:

Autobiographies, London: Macmillan, 1955.
Collected Plays, London: Macmillan, 1952.
Collected Poems, London: Macmillan, 1950.
Essays and Introductions, London: Macmillan, 1961.
Explorations, London: Macmillan, 1962.
Mythologies, London: Macmillan, 1959.
Senate Speeches, edited by Donald R. Pearce, London: Faber, 1960.
A Vision, London: Macmillan, 1961.
The Variorum Edition of the Poems of W. B. Yeats, edited by P. Allt and R. K. Alspach, New York: Macmillan, 1957.
The Letters of W. B. Yeats, edited by A. Wade, London: Hart-Davis, 1954.
Letters on Poetry from W. B. Yeats to Dorothy Wellesley, Oxford University Press, 1940.
W. B. Yeats and T. Sturge Moore: Their Correspondence, 1901-37, edited by Ursula Bridge, London: Routledge and Kegan Paul, 1953.

BIBLIOGRAPHY:

A. Wade, *A Bibliography of the Writings of W. B. Yeats* (second edition, revised), London: Hart Davis, 1958.

BIOGRAPHICAL AND CRITICAL STUDIES:

BOOKS:

Harold Bloom, *Yeats*, London: Oxford University Press, 1970.
Raymond Cowell, *W. B. Yeats* ('Literature in Perspective'), London: Evans, 1969.
Richard Ellmann, *The Identity of Yeats*, London: Macmillan, 1954.
Richard Ellmann, *Yeats: The Man and the Masks*, London: Macmillan, 1949.
Richard Ellmann, *Eminent Domain: Yeats among Wilde, Joyce, Pound and Auden*, New York: Oxford University Press, 1967.
Edward Engelberg, *The Vast Design: Patterns in W. B. Yeats's Aesthetic*, University of Toronto Press, 1964.
D. J. Gordon (ed.), *W. B. Yeats: Images of a Poet*, with essays by D. J. Gordon, Frank Kermode, Robin Skelton, Ian Fletcher, Manchester University Press, 1961.

Stephen Gwynn (ed.), *William Butler Yeats: Essays in Tribute*, New York: Kennikat Press, 1965. (Originally published by Macmillan in 1940 under the title: *Scattering Branches: Tributes to the Memory of W. B. Yeats.*)

T. W. Henn, *The Lonely Tower*, London: Methuen, 1950.

A. N. Jeffares, *W. B. Yeats: Man and Poet*, London: Routledge and Kegan Paul, 1949.

Vivienne Koch, *W. B. Yeats: The Tragic Phase*, London: Routledge and Kegan Paul, 1951.

Louis Macneice, *The Poetry of W. B. Yeats*, London: Faber and Faber, 1967. (Originally published by Oxford University Press, 1941.)

G. Melchiori, *The Whole Mystery of Art*, London: Routledge and Kegan Paul, 1960.

Thomas Parkinson, *W. B. Yeats: The Later Poetry*, California University Press, 1964.

Thomas Parkinson, *W. B. Yeats, Self-Critic: A Study of his Early Verse*, University of California Press, 1951.

G. B. Saul, *Prolegomena to the Study of Yeats's Poems*, Philadelphia: University of Pennsylvania Press, 1957.

Jon Stallworthy, *Between the Lines: Yeats's Poetry in the Making*, Oxford: The Clarendon Press, 1963.

A. G. Stock, *W. B. Yeats, His Poetry and Thought*, Oxford University Press, 1961.

Peter Ure, *Yeats* ('Writers and Critics'), Edinburgh and London: Oliver and Boyd, 1963.

T. R. Whitaker, *Swan and Shadow: Yeats's Dialogue with History*, University of North Carolina Press, 1964.

F. A. C. Wilson, *W. B. Yeats and Tradition*, London: Gollancz, 1958.

F. A. C. Wilson, *Yeats's Iconography*, London: Gollancz, 1960.

A. Zwerdling, *Yeats and the Heroic Ideal*, London: Peter Owen, 1966.

A. M. Garab, *Beyond Byzantium: The Last Phase of Yeats's Career*, De Kalb: Northern Illinois University Press, 1969.

ESSAYS:

John Bayley, 'W. B. Yeats', *The Romantic Survival: A Study in Poetic Evolution*, London: Constable, 1957, pp. 77–126.

R. P. Blackmur, 'W. B. Yeats: Between Myth and Philosophy', *Language as Gesture: Essays in Poetry*, London: George Allen and Unwin, 1954, pp. 105–23.

David Daiches, 'Yeats's Earlier Poems: Some Themes and Patterns', *More Literary Essays*, Edinburgh and London: Oliver and Boyd, 1968, pp. 133–49.

Denis Donoghue, 'Yeats and the Living Voice', *The Ordinary Universe*, London: Faber and Faber, 1968, pp. 125–45.

T. S. Eliot, 'Yeats', *On Poetry and Poets*, London: Faber and Faber, 1957, pp. 252–62.

Daniel Hoffman, ' "I Am of Ireland": Yeats the Ballad Poet', *Barbarous Knowledge: Myth in the Poetry of Yeats, Graves and Muir*, New York: Oxford University Press, 1967, pp. 27–59.

Frank Kermode, Part One, 'Dancer and Tree', *Romantic Image*, London: Routledge and Kegan Paul, 1961, pp. 1–103.

L. C. Knights, 'Poetry and Social Criticism: The Work of W. B. Yeats', *Explorations*, London: Chatto and Windus, 1946, pp. 170–85.

F. R. Leavis, 'Yeats: The Problem and the Challenge', F. R. Leavis and Q. D. Leavis, *Lectures in America*, London: Chatto and Windus, 1969, pp. 59–81.

Josephine Miles, 'The Classical Mode of Yeats', *Eras and Modes in English Poetry*, Berkeley and Los Angeles: University of California Press, 1957, pp. 178–202.

J. I. M. Stewart, 'Yeats', *Eight Modern Writers*, Oxford: The Clarendon Press, 1963, pp. 294–421.

ARTICLES:

Russell Alspach, 'Some Sources of Yeats's "The Wanderings of Oisin" ', *P.M.L.A.*, 1943, pp. 849–66.

W. H. Auden, 'Yeats as an Example', *Kenyon Review*, X, 1948, pp. 188–95.

Curtis Bradford, 'Yeats's Byzantium Poems: A Study of their Development', *P.M.L.A.*, LXXV, pp. 110–25.

Denis Donoghue, ' "The Vigour of Its Blood": Yeats's "Words for Music Perhaps" ', *Kenyon Review*, XXI, 1959, pp. 376–87.

Ian Fletcher, 'Explorations and Recoveries, II: Symons, Yeats and the Demonic Dance', *The London Magazine*, VII, 1960, pp. 46–60.

John Holloway, 'Yeats and the Penal Age', *Critical Quarterly*, VIII, 1966, pp. 58–66.

Walter E. Houghton, 'Yeats and Crazy Jane: The Hero in Old Age', *Modern Philology*, XL, 1942, pp. 316–29.

Laurence Lerner, 'W. B. Yeats: Poet and Crank', *Proceedings of the British Academy*, XLIX, 1963, Oxford University Press, 1964, pp. 49–67.

Graham Martin, 'Fine Manners, Liberal Speech: A Note on the Public Poetry of W. B. Yeats', *Essays in Criticism*, XI, 1961, pp. 40–59.

Jon Stallworthy, 'W. B. Yeats and Wilfred Owen', *Critical Quarterly*, XI, 3, 1969, pp. 199–214.

Peter Ure, 'Yeats's "Supernatural Songs" ', *Review of English Studies*, New Series VII, 1956, pp. 38–51.

CENTENARY TRIBUTES:

Of the three collections of essays in tribute, the following is probably the best:

Denis Donoghue and J. R. Mulryne (eds.), *An Honoured Guest: New Essays on W. B. Yeats*, London: Arnold, 1965.

COMMENTARIES:

A. N. Jeffares, *A Commentary on the Collected Poems of W. B. Yeats*, London: Macmillan, 1968.

J. Unterecker, *A Reader's Guide to William Butler Yeats*, London: Thames and Hudson, 1959.